The Struggle Against the State & Other Essays

by Nestor Makhno

edited by Alexandre Skirda

Library of Congress Cataloguing-in-Publication Data

Makhno, Nestor Ivanovich. 1889–1934.
   [Lutte contre l'Etat et autres écrits. English]
   The struggle against the state and other essays / by
Nestor Makhno ; edited by Alexandre Sirda.
      p.   cm.
   Includes biblographical references.
   ISBN 1-873176-78-3 (pbk.)
   1. Ukraine--History--Revolution. 1917–1921. 2.
Ukraine--History--1921-1944. 3. Anarchism. I. Skirda,
Alexandre. II. Title.
DK265.8.U4M27413 1995
947' 710841--dc20   95-40647
                                                         CIP

British Library Cataloguing in Publication Data

A catalogue record for this title is available from the
British Library.

First published in 1996 by

AK Press   AK Press
P.O. Box 12766   P.O. Box 40682
Edinburgh, Scotland   San Francisco, CA
EH8 9YE   94140-0682

The publication of this volume was in part made possible by the
generosity of Stefan Andreas Store, Chris Atton, Andy Hibbs,
Stephen John Adams, Bruno Ruhland, and the Friends of AK
Press.

Typeset and design donated by Freddie Baer.

TABLE OF CONTENTS

1. Great October in the Ukraine   1

2. On the 10th Anniversary of the
   Makhnovist Insurgent Movement in the Ukraine   6

3. On Defense of the Revolution   19

4. A Few Words on the National Question
   in the Ukraine   24

5. To the Jews of All Countries   28

6. The Makhovshchina and Anti-Semitism   32

7. In Memory of the Kronstadt Revolt   39

8. The Idea of Equality and the Bolsheviks   42

9. The Paths of "Proletarian" Power   46

10. "Soviet" Power — Its Present and Its Future   52

11. The Struggle Against the State   56

12. The First of May: Symbol of a New Era
    in the Life and Struggle of the Toilers   59

13. Anarchism and Our Times   61

14. Our Organization   64

15. On Revolutionary Discipline   67

16. The ABC of the Revolutionary Anarchist   70

17. Open Letter to the Spanish Anarchists   88

18. On the History of the Spanish Revolution of 1931
    and the Part Played by the Left and
    Right-Wing Socialists and the Anarchist   91

19. Bibliographical Afterword   99
    Alexandre Skirda

1. Great October in the Ukraine

The month of October 1917 is a great historical watershed in the Russian revolution. That watershed consists of the awakening of the toilers of town and country to their right to seize control of their own lives and their social and economic inheritance; the cultivation of the soil, the housing, the factories, the mines, transportation, and lastly the education which had hitherto been used to strip our ancestors of all these assets.

However, as we see it, it would be wide of the mark if we were to see all of the content of the Russian revolution encapsulated in October: in fact, the Russian revolution was hatched over the preceding months, a period during which the peasants in the countryside and the workers in the towns grasped the essential point. Indeed, the revolution of February 1917 came to be a symbol for the toilers of their economic and political liberation. However, they quickly noticed that the February revolution as it evolved adopted the degenerated format characteristic of the liberal bourgeoisie, and, as such, proved incapable of embarking upon a project of social action. Whereupon the toilers immediately cast off the restraints imposed by February and set about openly severing all their ties to its pseudo-revolutionary aspect and its objectives.

In the Ukraine, there were two facets to this activity. At the time, the urban proletariat, in view of the meagerness of the anarchists' influence upon it on the one hand, and lack of information about the real political policies and domestic issues in the country on the other, reckoned that hoisting the Bolsheviks into power had become the most pressing necessity of the battle that had been joined for the pursuance of the revolution, if the coalition of Right Social Revolutionaries with the bourgeoisie was to be ousted.

Meanwhile, in the countryside, and especially in the Zaporozhe area of the Ukraine, where the autocracy had never quite managed to extirpate the spirit of freedom, the toiling revolutionary peasantry took it as its most over-riding and most basic duty to resort to direct revolution-ary action in order to rid themselves as quickly as possible of the pomeshchiks and kulaks, being persuaded that this liberation would speed their victory against the socialist-bourgeois coalition.

This is the reason why the Ukrainian peasants went on the offensive, seizing the bourgeoisie's weaponry (par-ticularly at the time of putschist General Kornilov's march on Petrograd in August 1917) and then refusing to pay the second annual installment of land levies to the big land-lords and kulaks. (The agents of the coalition tried in fact to wrest the land from the peasants, in order to hold it for the estate-owners, allegedly in deference to the government's adherence to the status quo pending the convening of the Constituent Assembly which would de-cide on the matter).

The peasants then got up and seized the estates and livestock of the pomeshchiks, kulaks, monasteries and State holdings: in so doing, they always set up local committees to manage these assets, with an eye to sharing them out among the various villages and communes.

An instinctive anarchism clearly illumined all the plans of the Ukraine's toiling peasantry, which gave vent to an undisguised hatred of all State authority, a feeling accompanied by a plain ambition to liberate themselves. The latter, indeed, is very strong in the peasants: in essence it boils down to, first, getting rid of the bourgeois authori-ties like the gendarmerie, the magistrates sent out by the central authorities, etc. This was put into practice in many regions in the Ukraine. There are examples aplenty of the way in which the peasants in the provinces of Ekaterinoslav, Kherson, Poltava, Kharkov and part of Tavripol drove the gendarmerie out of their villages, or even stripped it of the right to make arrests without the say-so of the peasant committees and village assemblies. The gendarmes wound up as simply the bearers of the decisions these made. It was not long before the magistrates were reduced to like business.

The peasants themselves sat in judgment of all offenses and disputes at village assemblies or at special meetings, thereby denying all jurisdictional rights to the magistrates appointed by the central authorities. These magistrates sometimes fell so far from grace that they were often forced to flee or go into hiding.

Such an approach by the peasants to their individual and social rights naturally inclined them to fear lest the slogan "All power to the soviets" turn into a State power: these fears were perhaps less plainly evident among the urban proletariat, which was more under the sway of the social democrats and Bolsheviks.

To the peasants, the power of local soviets meant the conversion of those bodies into autonomous territorial units, on the basis of the revolutionary association and socio-economic self-direction of the toilers with an eye to the construction of a new society. Placing that sort of construction upon that slogan, the peasants applied it literally, expanded upon it and defended it against the trespasses of the Right SRs, Cadets (liberals) and the monarchist counter-revolutionaries.

Thus October had not yet happened when the peasants jumped the gun by refusing in many regions to pay the farm rents to the pomeshchiks and kulaks, then, having collectively seized the latter's land and livestock, despatching delegates to the urban proletariat to come to some arrangement with it regarding the seizure of the factories and firms, the aim being to establish fraternal connections and, jointly, build the new, free society of toilers.

At this point, the practical implementation of the ideas of "Great October" had not yet been espoused by those who would later subscribe to it, the Bolsheviks and the Left SRs: it was even harshly criticized by their groups, organizations and central committees. On the other hand, as far as the Ukrainian peasants were concerned, Great October, and especially the status it was afforded in political chronology, looked very much like a chapter they had long since moved on from.

During the events in October, the proletariat of Petrograd, Moscow and other large cities, as well as the soldiers and the peasants adjacent to the towns, under the influence of anarchists, Bolsheviks and Left SRs, merely regularized and gave more precise political expression to that for which the revolutionary peasantry of many areas of the Ukraine had begun to struggle actively as early as the month of August 1917, and that in highly favorable conditions, enjoying, as they had, the backing of the urban proletariat.

The repercussions of the proletariat's version of October reached the Ukraine a month and a half later. The intent behind it was evident at first from the appeals from the delegates from the soviets and parties, then from the decrees of the Soviet of People's Commissars, about which the Ukrainian peasants were diffident, having had no part in their appointments.

It was then that groups of Red Guards showed up in the Ukraine, coming largely from Russia, and attacking the towns and communications centers controlled by the Cossacks of the Ukrainian Central Rada. The latter was so infected by chauvinism that it found it impossible to understand that of the laboring population of the country could relate to their brethren from Russia, nor, above all, appreciate the revolutionary spirit at large among the toiling population which stood ready to fight for its social and political independence.

In offering this analysis of Great October on this, the occasion of its tenth anniversary, we ought to stress that what we accomplished in the Ukraine was perfectly in tune, in late 1917, with the actions of the revolutionary workers in Petrograd, Moscow and other great cities in Russia.

Whilst taking note of the revolutionary faith and enthusiasm displayed by the countryside of the Ukraine long before October, we respect and hold in every bit as high regard the determination and vigor displayed by the Russian workers, peasants and soldiers during the events of October.

In reviewing the past, we cannot let the present go unremarked, for it is bound up with October one way or another. Also, we can only state our profound distress at the fact that, after ten years, the ideas that were fully expressed in October are still the objects of derision from the very people that have come to power and governed Russia since in the name of those ideas.

We express our saddened solidarity to all who fought for the triumph of October and are currently rotting in prisons and concentration camps. Their sufferings under torture and famine have reached us and compel us to feel a profound sorrow, on this the tenth anniversary of October, in place of the usual joy.

As a matter of revolutionary duty, we raise our voice once again to cry across the borders of the USSR:

Give the sons of October their freedom, give them back their rights to organize and to spread their ideas!

In the absence of freedom, and rights for the toilers and revolutionary militants, the USSR is suffocating and doing to death the best part of itself. Its enemies are delighted by this and are making preparations world-wide, with the aid of all possible means, to extirpate the revolution and, with it, the USSR.

Dyelo Truda No 29, October 1927, pp. 9-11.

2. On the 10th Anniversary of the Makhnovist Insurgent Movement in the Ukraine

As we know, the Bolshevik leaders' shameful betrayal of the ideas of the October Revolution led the entire Bolshevik party and its 'proletarian revolutionary' authority, once in place all across the country, to conclude a disgraceful peace with the German Kaiser Wilhelm II and the Austrian Emperor, Karl, followed by an even more deplorable struggle inside the country against anarchism, first of all, and then against the Left Social Revolutionaries and socialism in general. In June 1918, I met with Lenin in the Kremlin, at the instigation of Sverdlov, the then chairman of the All-Russian Executive Committee of the Soviets. Citing my mandate as head of the Revolutionary Defense Committee in the Gulyai-Polye region, I briefed Lenin on the unequal fight waged by the revolutionary forces in the Ukraine against the Austro-German invaders and their allies on the Ukrainian Central Rada: he discussed this with me and, having noted my fanatical peasant attachment to the revolution and to the anarchist ideas it encapsulated, he assured me that the soviet authorities had initiated a struggle in the urban centers of the revolution, not against anarchism per se, but rather against the bandits who professed to be its followers:

> With those anarchists engaged in organized revolutionary activity, like the ones you have just

been talking about, our Bolshevik party and I myself will always be able to speak the same language with an eye to building a joint revolutionary front. . . . It is quite another matter with the social-traitors who are the real enemies of the genuine emancipation of the proletariat and the poor peasantry: with regard to them, my attitude will always be unbending: I am their enemy.

The degree of guile and hypocrisy that Lenin exhibited on that occasion is but rarely encountered in a master-politician. By that point the Bolshevik authorities had already orchestrated repression against anarchism, in the very deliberate intention of discrediting it in the country. Lenin's Bolshevism had placed an X against every free revolutionary organization and anarchism alone was still enough of a danger to it, for, had it but learned to act in an organized and strictly consistent way among the broad masses of the workers and peasants, so as to steer them to victory in political and strategic terms, anarchism alone could have conjured up all that was healthy and utterly committed to the revolution in the country and expected to make the ideas of freedom, equality and free labor practical living realities through its struggle.

Let it be noted that, vis-a-vis socialists, Lenin employed equally insulting tones. . . . The Bolshevik authorities' offensive against anarchism and socialism rendered great service at that juncture to the foreign counter-revolutionaries, whose troops were making easy headway into revolutionary territory in the Ukraine and swiftly ousting all the revolutionary fighting detachments led by anarchists, Social Revolutionaries or indeed by the odd Bolshevik.

Thanks to this disgraceful treachery by the Bolshevik leaders, the counter-revolution was able in short order to paralyze all revolutionary links between the towns and villages of the Ukraine, before turning to massive repression. In this way, the Ukrainian revolution found itself quite unexpectedly before the gallows of its executioners and was well chastened in this first stage of its development. . . .

Those were dark days filled with bloody horrors. Under the agreements reached with the Central Emperors, the Bolshevik leaders evacuated all the well armed and disciplined revolutionary detachments of Russian workers from the Ukraine, at a time when the Ukrainian workers were poorly armed, direly equipped and compelled to fall back in the wake of their Russian brethren, powerless to confront the revolution's enemies. In sometimes bloody skirmishing, they clashed with the Bolshevik authorities who were refusing them entry into Russia with their weaponry. It was in those days, when all seemed lost, that the revolutionary peasants, united around the libertarian communist group in Gulyai-Polye and dispersed in numerous groups and detachments, also retreated towards Russia, where, they reckoned, the revolution was still on course and might help them recover the strength they needed to tackle the counter-revolutionary invaders again. . . . Unfortunately, even at that stage in the revolution, the Bolshevik leadership could be seen turning clearly against all that was healthy and revolutionary in the toiling masses, who were systematically denigrated to the benefit of their party privileges and the runaway counter-revolution lurking behind them. On the approaches to the town of Taganrog, the Bolshevik authorities set up ambushes of independent revolutionary groups and detachments in the intention of stripping them of their weapons. This circumstance led the forces from the proud revolutionary region of Gulyai-Polye to break up into tiny groups, some of which made their way home surreptitiously, whilst others gathered equally clandestinely in Taganrog to determine what should be done thereafter. . . .

In Taganrog, I was commissioned along with Veretelnikov (by the group of comrades there) to organize a conference. It went ahead. Its resolutions were short but to the point, in that no participant had decided to continue the fall-back. With the exception of myself, Veretelnikov and three other comrades, all the others decided to rejoin the front lines and work away there discreetly among the peasantry, with the utmost caution. My four colleagues and I were commissioned by the conference to spend two or three months in Moscow, Petrograd and Kronstadt so as to familiarize ourselves with the progress of the revolution in those revolutionary centers, before returning to the Ukraine by the first days of July, to the areas where it had been determined that free Revolutionary Defense battalions were to be organized, the clear intention being not just to fight but also to win.

Alone of my comrades, I was able to make it back to the Ukraine in time: there the Austro-Germans and their stooge, the Hetman Skoropadsky, were indulging their political and economic whims. I found but few of my old comrades there, most of them having been killed or jailed pending execution. Deeply convinced of the necessity of carrying out the task with which I had been entrusted by the Taganrog conference, I made contact with the region's peasants with an eye to choosing from among them persons disposed to commit themselves to the struggle. I had meetings with numerous peasant men and women whom I had earlier had occasion to bring around to my way of thinking. With their help, I managed to trace certain of my comrades who had escaped the arrests and shootings by the Austro-Germans and the executioners of the revolution, and who were still determined to fight back. Not waiting for our comrades to return from Russia, and undeterred by the risks involved in our sojourns in villages, which were forever subject to raids and search operations by the occupiers and their allies, often followed by the arrest and execution of our most active comrades, we managed quite quickly to get up and running an organization designed to pave the way to the revolutionary uprising of the peasant masses against the Hetman and his feudal-agrarian regime, as well as against their protectors, the Austro-Hungarian-German troops. Our language at the time went like this:

Peasants, workers and you, the working intelligentsia! Support the rebirth and expansion of the revolution as the most reliable weapon in the fight against Capital and the State! Support the creation and strengthening of a free society of workers in your life-time, our common objective! You must organize yourselves, form partisan style revolutionary combat detachments and battalions from among your ranks, then rise up, set upon the Hetman and the Austro-German emperors — those who sent their savage counter-revolutionary armies against us — and at all costs defeat these executioners of the revolution and of freedom . . . !

The toiling masses listened to us and they understood us. Villages and hamlets far removed from Gulyai-Polye itself sent their delegates to see us, seeking to join the anarchist group and then bring one of its members back with them for discussions and to prepare the way for the uprising. At that time I used to travel either alone or with three or four comrades: I held clandestine meetings with the peasants from these villages and districts. After two months of this demanding and dogged propaganda and organizing effort, carried out by the region's peasants, our Gulyai-Polye libertarian communist group observed that a swarm of workers stood ready to follow its lead, among them many armed rebels determined to put an end to the economic and political arbitrariness of the Hetman and the Austro-German junkers.

I recall one time when the delegates from the units which we had already organized spent a week touring the region in an attempt to link up with me. I who was the man the bourgeoisie and the Austro-German command loved to hate. For my part, I too traveled around from village to village in the company of two or three comrades, carrying out my organizing drive. They manage to link up with me and on behalf of those who had sent them, they asked me not to postpone the unleashing of the general armed insurrection against the revolution's enemies to some date deemed more opportune. They informed me:

(. . .) Nestor Ivanovitch, come back to Gulyai-Polye to raise its inhabitants in revolt! If they rise, all villages, districts and regions will follow suit. With your band of agitator comrades, by dint of your zealous efforts, you have already brought your township of Gulyai-Polye to a rare fever pitch of revolutionary revolt against the Hetman and the Austro-Germans. Your summons, issued from rebel Gulyai-Polye, will do more for the work of insurrection for which we will all prepare ourselves, than all these weeks you have spent touring the villages to prepare the way for this undertaking with verbal agitation, exposing your very life to the greatest risks.

I did not let myself be swayed by such trust and the tribute paid to our group and to me personally. Devoid of any revolutionary vanity, I strove to inculcate the same precept into my friends and the masses among whom we were operating; it was a matter of retaining the lucidity and understanding that we had conjured into existence for the prosecution of the revolution, which had been stalled for the time being by the counter-revolutionary executioners.

My travels through the revolutionary centers of Russia, the experiences and observations I had garnered from them, had all opened my eyes to a lot of things. It was for all these reasons that along with my friends from the Gulyai-Polye libertarian communist group, I had devoted myself to the organizing of the peasant uprising against the enemies of the revolution and been scrupulously watchful lest any underplaying of our role make us forgetful of the real tasks that had fallen to our lot. Thus to all the importunate demands from peasants that the rising be unleashed, I continually repeated, in my capacity as instigator and chief of the insurrection:

Down your way, are all your forces connected enough with your group in organizational terms? Have you all understood that the insurrection must erupt everywhere at the same time, even though the different districts are far from one another?

— If you have realized that, it would not be a waste of time to reflect one more time on the most productive way of launching our armed struggle. Especially as we are a long way from having access to the same technical resources as our enemies, when indeed our first blows we strike will have to secure us a number of rifles and artillery pieces, as well as twenty cartridges and shells for each rifle and cannon.

— Such a success will be doubly satisfying to us, for we shall promptly derive greater determination from it, politically, organizationally and in fighting terms alike. Following that initial success, all our partisan detachments will fall upon the enemy from every side, thereby sowing the most utter confusion among the Austro-German command and the Hetman's government, in our Lower Dniepr and Donet Basin region at any rate. Then, during the summer, events should take a more favorable turn for us and allow us to step up our struggle even further.

These were terms in which we anarchist peasants addressed the toiling masses at a time of dire difficulty for the revolution and our movement's ideas. The question might be posed: Why were we so very, perhaps even unduly, cautious about our influence over the masses, when they were the first to call for an uprising against the oppressors? Why, it might be asked, when we were naturally carried away by the spirit of revolt, had we not simply placed ourselves at the head of these masses, so imbued with the elements unleashed by the revolutionary anarchist tempest which was quite bereft of ulterior political motives? Now this might seem odd, but our attitude was determined solely by the circumstances of the time especially by those that in the libertarian movement are only rarely acknowledged as crucial. Indeed, for an active revolutionary vanguard, this was a time of great strain, for it required painstaking preparation of the uprising. Our Gulyai-Polye libertarian communist group was just such a vanguard and events led it to pose the question of whether it should assume complete responsibility for leading the movement of the seething toiling masses or surrender that role to someone of these parties with their ready made programs and which also had access to direct support from the 'revolutionary' Bolshevik government in Moscow?

That question made life difficult for our group, especially as in such busy times there was no question of invoking anarchism's abstract notions with their rejection of disciplined organization of revolutionary forces, the upshot of which was that anarchists would have found themselves isolated in revolutionary activity and stranded by the very existence of the creative and productive part that was in principle theirs to play. For all the revolutionary ardor and first hand experience that impelled us to spare no effort to thwart the counter-revolution, we aspired to act as anarchists with an abiding faith in the correctness of the doctrine's fundamental principles. However, we were well aware of the disorganization prevailing within the anarchist movement, doing it considerable damage and playing into the hands of the Bolsheviks and the Left Social Revolutionaries. We also realized that this habitual disorganization was a lot more firmly rooted among most anarchists than the positive aspects of their teaching and that as a result, this disorganization was so much the chief trait of the anarchist movement that it could not be either comprehended or supported by the masses, who had no desire to go blindly to their deaths in some pointless struggle.

We had furnished the best possible solution to this problem by organizing the insurrection directly and paying no heed to the possible carping from our fellow-believers regarding this vanguardist stance which they saw as ill suited to anarchist teachings. Thus in practice we disposed of such inconsequential blather that was so damaging to our cause and concentrated instead on seeing the struggle through to complete victory. However, this required that revolutionary anarchism, if it sought to play its part properly and fulfill its active task in contemporary revolutions, face up to immense demands of an organizational nature whether in the training of its personnel or in defining its dynamic role in the early days of the revolution when the toiling masses were often groping their way.

Cognizant of the atomization of anarchist circles and their semi-legal existence towns and cities, where the Bolsheviks were set upon destroying them or making them into auxiliaries of the Bolshevik authorities, we peasant anarchists operated in the countryside in such a way as to ensure that the voice of our anarchist movement got a hearing there and to draw out all that was best and healthiest from the towns so as to raise the flag of revolt against the Hetman and his Austro-German sponsors.

It was with this in mind that our group schooled the region's toiling peasantry whilst not surrendering one iota of basic anarchist principles: it boosted the armed struggle and drafted the political program of the insurgent movement which soon came to known everywhere as the "Batko Makhno revolutionary units."

So strong and productive were the group's influence and my own that no political force inimical to anarchism, particularly the socialist parties, had any chance of prevailing against them in the minds of the insurgent masses, who heeded neither their slogans nor indeed the speechifying of their orators. Makhno's words and those of the members of the Gulyai-Polye libertarian communist peasant group regarding the freedom and independence of workers vis-a-vis Capital and its servant, the State, were taken on board by the masses and their import regarded as the basis for the struggle to replace the noxious organization of bourgeois capitalist society by the free organization of toilers.

It was in the name of that objective that the peasant masses created a mighty armed force, placed it under the command of the Staff organized by the Gulyai-Polye libertarian group and thereafter sustained it on a permanent basis. These economic and psychological ties were never broken after that, with the toiling population unstintingly rallying around the movement even in its darkest days, keeping it supplied with manpower and provisions.

In this way the Gulyai-Polye region quickly became a land apart, for all statist tendencies were banished from its self-organization. The savage hordes of Austro-Germans who had hitherto known no restraint upon their arbitrariness, were smashed and disarmed, with their weaponry being taken over by the movement.

Consequently these troops began to scurry out of the region: as for the Hetman Skoropadsky's men, some were hanged, others driven out. The Bolshevik government soon learned of the existence of this proud region as well as of the anarchists who were the inspiration behind its insurgent movement. It was at this point that Bolshevik newspapers used to make no bones about citing the name of Makhno on their front pages, reporting daily the successes of the campaign waged under his leadership.

The insurgent movement forged ahead. Having routed the Austro-Germans, then driven out the Hetman's men from a succession of districts in the Ukraine, it encountered the beginnings of the Denikinist backlash and the Ukrainian Directory — better known as the 'Petliurovshchina' — against which they promptly deployed all their efforts under the direction of the anarchist peasants, as ever, they being the revolution's most devoted sons. A broad front was built up against these new foes and heroic military operations conducted in the interests of the revolution and a new, free society of toilers.

Against this backdrop, the anarchist peasants organized the insurgent movement of the Ukraine's toilers, which subsequently grew into the Makhnovist movement. In light of this summary, albeit an incomplete one, those who have encountered the fairy tales peddled by the enemies of the Makhnovshchina and on occasion by certain of its "friends," daring to suggest that this grassroots movement had no ideology, that its doctrinal and political inspirations alike were drawn from outside, will be in a position to conclude that such allegations are utterly without foundation.

The guides of the movement, as well as the toiling peasant masses who backed it from start to finish, are well aware that it was organized by the Gulyai-Polye libertarian communist group and that it always enshrined the anarchist expectations of those who were not misled by revolutionary verbalism nor by the chaotic tendencies and irresponsible mentality so frequently encountered in the towns. The inspirations and organizers of the insurgent movement such as the Karetnik brothers, Alexis Marchenko, the Semenyuta brothers, the Domashenko brothers, the Makhno brothers, Lyuty, Zuichenko, Korostelev, Troyan, Danilov, Tykhenko, Moshtchenko, A. Chubenko and lots of others, were all anarchists. Many of them had been active among the peasants back in 1906-1907 and were in fact the movement's pioneers. It was they, along with others from inside the movement, who sustained it in terms of its political ideas as well as of its military and strategic organization. Any help from anarchist organizations, the ones closest in terms of their thinking, was eagerly awaited but to our great regret was never forthcoming in an organizational way. For the first nine months of its military operations against the revolution's enemies, the anarchist movement saw nothing from what should have been its natural friends, the urban anarchists. It was only later that some came out to join it, in an individual capacity mainly, especially those who were indebted to the movement for their release from enemy hands. The libertarian communist group from Ivanovo-Vosnessensk, headed by comrades Makeyev and A. Chernyakov, was the only one to throw in its lot with the Makhnovist movement, in an organizational way. It rendered it needed and significant help, but unfortunately only temporarily, for most of its members drifted away a short time later.

Throughout these tough years of an unequal, exacting and (politically and historically) telling struggle, the Makhnovist movement drew all its sustenance exclusively from its own internal resources. This, I am convinced, was the essential reason why it was able to stick staunchly to its revolutionary post and, despite the endless fighting due to its being encircled at all times, the reason why it followed no other path but that of anarchism and social revolution.

Abiding by its anarchist ideas, forbidding the State and its supporters from interfering with the self-direction of the urban and rural toilers in their endeavors to build a free society, the Makhnovist movement could not of course expect any help from the statist political parties: on the other hand, it was entitled to look for such help to the anarchist organizations in the towns, which help, unfortunately, never came. Disorganizational practices were so deep rooted at that time among the bulk of the anarchists as to blind them to what was going on in the countryside. On the whole, they failed to notice or to grasp in time the anarchist spirit abroad in the peasantry, and, as a result to bring their influence to bear on the urban workers' organizations. Having taken note of this dereliction, the Makhnovist movement thus has no reason to feel grateful for this defect in the anarchists' urban organizations. Out of this appreciation arose its faith in the rightness of the positions it adopted regarding the revolutionary endeavor. It was able to abide firmly by these, which enabled it to fight on for so many years whilst relying solely upon its own resources. In thereby living up to its revolutionary duty, which was both onerous and crucial, the Makhnovist movement made but one serious mistake: it joined forces with Bolshevism to wage a joint campaign against Wrangel and the Entente. While that compact lasted, and it was certainly valuable practically and psychologically for the success of the revolution, the Makhnovist movement was mistaken about the Bolsheviks' revolutionism and failed to take preventive steps in time against their treachery. The Bolsheviks treacherously attacked it, with the assistance of all their "soldiery" and, albeit with great difficulty, defeated it for a time.

From *Djelo Truda* No. 44-45, January/February 1928, pp. 3-7.

3. ON DEFENSE OF THE REVOLUTION

Within the context of the debate that has taken place among our comrades from many lands regarding the *Draft Platform of the General Union of Anarchists*, published by the group of Russian anarchists abroad, I have been asked from several quarters to write a piece specifically devoted to the issue of the defense of the revolution. I shall strive to deal with it most diligently, but, before I do, I think I have a duty to inform comrades that this is not the central issue of the *Draft Platform*: the crux of it is the necessity of achieving the most consistent unity in our libertarian communist ranks. That portion asks only for amendment and completion before implementation. Otherwise, if we do not strive to marshal our forces, our movement will be condemned to succumb once and for all to the influences of liberals and opportunists who haunt our circles, if not outright speculators and political adventurers, who, at best, can prattle on and on but are incapable of fighting on the ground for the attainment of our great objectives. The latter can only happen if we carry along with us all who instinctively believe in the rightness of our struggle and who seek to achieve the widest possible freedom and independence through revolution, so as to build a new life and a new society, wherein the individual may at last and unimpeded exercise his creative drive on behalf of the general good.

As far as the specific issue of defense of the revolution goes, I shall be relying upon my first-hand experiences during the Russian revolution in the Ukraine, in the course of that unequal, but decisive struggle waged by the revolutionary movement of the Ukrainian toilers. Those experiences taught me, first, that defense of the revolution is directly bound up with its offensive against the Counter-revolution: secondly, its expansion and its intensity are at all times conditioned by the resistance of the counter-revolutionaries: thirdly, what follows from the above, namely that revolutionary actions are closely dependent on the political content, structure and organizational methods adopted by the armed revolutionary detachments, who are obliged to confront conventional, counter-revolutionary armies along a huge front.

In its fight against its enemies, the Russian revolution at first began by organizing Red Guard detachments under the leadership of the Bolsheviks. It was very quickly spotted that these failed to withstand the pressures from enemy troops, to be specific, the German, Austrian and Hungarian expeditionary corps, for the simple reason that, most of the time, they operated without any overall operational guide-lines. That is why the Bolsheviks turned in the spring of 1918 to the organization of a Red Army.

It was then that we issued the call to form "free battalions" of Ukrainian toilers. It quickly transpired that that organization was powerless to survive internal provocations of every sort, given that, without adequate vetting, political or social, it took in all volunteers provided only that they wanted to take up their weapons and fight. This was why the armed units established by that organization were treacherously delivered to the enemy, a fact that prevented it from seeing through its historical mission in the fight against the foreign counter-revolution.

However, following that initial set-back to the "free battalions" organization — which might be described as fighting units of the revolution's first line of defense — we did not lose our heads. The organization was somewhat overhauled in its format: the battalions were complemented by light partisan detachments of a mixed type, that is, comprising infantry and cavalry alike. The task of these detachments was to operate far behind the enemy's lines. This organization proved itself during its operations against the Austro-German expeditionary forces and the bands of the Hetman Skoropadsky, their ally, during the late summer and autumn of 1918.

Sticking to that form of organizing the defense of the revolution, the Ukrainian toilers were able to wrest from the clutches of the counter-revolutionaries the noose that the latter had thrown around the revolution in the Ukraine. What is more, not content with defending the revolution, they followed it through as fully as they could.*

As the internal counter-revolution spread inside the country, it received aid from other countries, not just in the form of arms and munitions but also in the shape of troops. Despite that, our organization of the defense of the revolution also expanded in size and at the same time, as the need arose, adopted a new format and more suitable fighting methods.

We know that the most perilous counter-revolutionary front at that time was manned by the army of General Denikin: however, the insurgent movement held its own against him for five to six months. A fair number of the

---

*Note — At that time, the Bolsheviks had no military unit in the Ukraine: not until much later did their first fighting units arrive from Russia whereupon they occupied a front parallel to ours, apparently striving to join up with the Ukrainian toilers, who were organized autonomously and above all without their statist supervision, but in fact they set to work in an underhand fashion to break them up and eliminate them for their own advantage. In order to encompass their goal, the Bolsheviks shrank from nothing, going so far as to directly sabotage the support they were pledged to provide in the form of munitions and shells: this at the very moment when we were mounting a broad offensive all along our front, the success of which hinged primarily upon the fire-power of our artillery and our machine-guns, when we were in fact tremendously short of munitions.

best Denikinist commanders came to grief against our units which had no weapons other than those taken from the enemy. Our organization made a large contribution to that: without trampling on the autonomy of the fighting units, it reorganized them into regiments and brigades coordinated by a common operational Staff. It is true that the establishment of the latter was feasible only thanks to the appreciation by the toiling revolutionary masses serving on the front lines facing the enemy as well as behind his lines, of the necessity of a single military command. Furthermore, still under the influence of our libertarian communist peasant group from Gulyai-Polye, the toilers also saw to it that every individual was awarded equal rights to take part in the construction of the new society, in every sphere, including the obligation to defend its gains.

Thus, whilst the Denikin front threatened the very life of the libertarian revolution which was being watched with a lively interest by the population at large, the revolutionary toilers came together on the basis of our organizational notion of defense of the revolution, making that their own and they bolstered the insurgent army with a regular influx of fresh combatants to relieve the wounded and the weary.

Elsewhere, the practical requirements of the struggle induced our movement to establish an operational and organizational Staff to share the oversight of all the fighting units. It is because of this practice that I find myself unable to subscribe to the view that revolutionary anarchists reject the need for such a Staff to oversee the armed revolutionary struggle strategically. I am convinced that any revolutionary anarchist finding himself in the same circumstances as those I encountered in the civil war in the Ukraine will, of necessity, be impelled to do as we did. If, in the course of the coming authentic social revolution, there are anarchists who rebut these organizational principles, then in our movement we will have only empty chatterers or dead-weight, harmful elements who will be rejected in short order.

In tackling the resolution of the matter of the revolution's defense, anarchists must unceasingly look to the social character of libertarian communism. Faced with a mass revolutionary movement, we have to acknowledge the need to organize that and endow it with means worthy of it, then throw ourselves into it whole-heartedly. Otherwise, if we appear to be dreamers and utopians, then we must not hamper the toilers' struggle, in particular those who follow the state socialists. Beyond the shadow of a doubt, anarchism is and remains a revolutionary social movement and that is why I am and always will be an advocate of its having a well articulated organization and support the establishment, come the revolution, of battalions, regiments, brigades and divisions designed to amalgamate, at certain times, into one common army, under a single regional command in the shape of supervisory organizational Staffs. The task of the latter will be, according to the requirements and conditions of the struggle, to draw up a federative operational plan, co-ordinating the actions of regional armies, so as to bring to a successful conclusion the fighting conducted on all fronts against the armed counter-revolution.

The matter of the defence of the revolution is no easy matter: it may require very great organisational commitment from the revolutionary masses. Anarchists must realise that and stand by to assist them in that undertaking.

Dyelo Truda No 25, June 1927, pp. 1 3-14.

4. A Few Words on the National Question in the Ukraine

In the wake of the abolition of tsarist despotism at the time of the 1917 revolution, prospects of new, free relations between peoples hitherto in subjection beneath the violent yoke of the Russian State, appeared on the horizons of the world of Labor. The notion of complete self-determination, up to and including a complete break with the Russian State, thus emerged naturally among these peoples. Groups of every persuasion sprang up among the Ukrainian population by the dozen: each of them had its own outlook and interpreted the idea of self-determination according to its own factional interests. All in all, the toiling masses of the Ukraine did not identify with these groups and did not join them.

Over seven years have elapsed since, and the Ukrainian toilers' line on the notion of self-determination has developed and their understanding increased. Now they identified with it and they displayed this often in their lifestyle. Thus, for example, they asserted their rights to use their own language and their entitlement to their own culture, which had been regarded prior to the revolution as anathema. They also asserted their right to conform in their lives to their own way of life and specific customs. In the aim of building an independent Ukrainian State, certain statist gentlemen would dearly love to arrogate to themselves all natural manifestations of Ukrainian reality, against which the Bolsheviks, by the way, are powerless to fight, for all their omnipotence. However, these statist gentlemen cannot seem to carry the broad masses of toilers with them, much less mobilize them in this way for a struggle against the oppressive Bolshevik party. The healthy instincts of the Ukrainian toilers and their baleful life under the Bolshevik yoke has not made them oblivious of the State danger in general. For that reason, they shun the chauvinist trend and do not mix it up with their social aspirations, rather seeking their own road to emancipation.

There is food there for serious thought on the part of all Ukrainian revolutionaries and for libertarian communists in particular, if they aim after this to engage in consistent work among the Ukrainian toilers.

Such work, though, cannot be conducted along the same lines as in the years 1918-1920, for the reality in the country has altered a lot. Then, the Ukrainian laboring population, which had played such a significant part in crushing all of the bourgeoisie's mercenaries — Denikin, Petliura and Wrangel — could never have dreamed that, at the far end of the revolution, it would find itself so ignominiously deceived and exploited by the Bolsheviks.

Those were the days when we were all fighting against the restoration of the tsarist order. There was not enough time then to scrutinize and vet all the "blow-ins" showing up to join the struggle. Faith in the revolution overruled all second thoughts about the mettle of these "blow-ins" or the questions that might have been raised about them; should they be counted as friends or foes? At the time, the toilers were on the move against the counter-revolution, heedful only of those who showed up to share their front ranks in confronting death fearlessly in defense of the revolution.

Later, the psychology of the Ukrainian toilers changed a lot: they had had the time to familiarize themselves to saturation point with these "blow-ins" to their cause, and thereafter were more critical in their accounting of what they had won through the revolution, or at least what remains of that. Behind these "blow-ins" they recognize their outright enemies, even though these Ukrainianized themselves and wave the flag of socialism, for, in actuality, they watch them operate in such a way as to add to the exploitation of Labor. They are clear in their minds that it was this caste of socialists, voracious exploiters, that stripped them of all their revolutionary gains. In short, as far as they are concerned it is something akin to the Austro-German occupation camouflaged behind all manner of Bolshevik sleight of hand.

This disguised occupation prompts from the masses a certain chauvinist backlash directed against the "blow-ins". Not for nothing do these Bolshevik gentlemen govern the Ukraine from Moscow, hiding behind their Ukrainian cat's paws: it is the growing hatred from the Ukrainian masses that has commended this course to them. It is the very nature of the Bolshevik despotism that is driving the Ukrainian toilers to search for ways of overthrowing it and making progress towards a new and truly free society. The Bolsheviks are not resting on their laurels either and are striving to adapt at all costs to Ukrainian reality. In 1923, they ended up like lost sheep: since which they have modified their tactics and wasted no time in getting to grips with Ukrainian reality. Furthermore, they have wasted no time in associating the fate of Bolshevism with that of nationalism, and they have, in pursuance of this, added specific articles to the 'Constitution of the USSR', affording every component people of that Union full rights of self-determination, indeed of secession. All of which is, of course, mere show. How is this attitude of the Bolsheviks going to develop? The next few years will tell. Anarchists' approach to the reality of the Ukraine now should take due account of these new factors — the Ukrainian toilers' hatred for the "blow-ins" of nationalist Bolshevism. By our reckoning, their chief task today consists of explaining to the masses that the root of all evil is not some "blow-in" authorities, but all authority in general. The history of recent years will afford considerable weight to their argument, for the Ukraine has seen a parade of all manner of authorities and, when all is said and done, these have been as indistinguishable one from another as peas in a pod. We must demonstrate that a "blow-in" State power and an "independent" State power amount to just about equal in value and that the toilers have nothing to gain from either: they should focus all their attention elsewhere: on destroying the nests of the State apparatus and replacing these with worker and peasant bodies for social and economic self-direction.

In spite of everything, in broaching the national question, we should not overlook the latest developments in the Ukraine. Ukrainian is being spoken now, and by virtue of the new nationalist trend, outsiders who do not speak the local language are scarcely listened to. This is an ethnic thing that ought to be kept in the forefront of our minds. Whereas, up to now, anarchists have enjoyed only a feeble audience among the Ukrainian peasantry, that was because they were concentrated above all in the towns and, what is more, did not use the national tongue of the Ukrainian countryside.

Ukrainian life is filled with all sorts of possibilities, especially the potential for a mass revolutionary movement. Anarchists have a great chance of influencing that movement, indeed becoming its mentors, provided only that they appreciate the diversity of real life and espouse a position to wage a single-minded, direct and declared fight against those forces hostile to the toilers which might have ensconced themselves there. That is a task that cannot be accomplished without a large and powerful Ukrainian anarchist organization. It is for Ukrainian anarchists to give that some serious thought, starting now.

Dyelo Truda No 19, December 1928.

5. To the Jews of All Countries

Jewish citizens! In my first "Appeal to Jews", published in the French libertarian newspaper, *Le Libertaire*, I asked Jews in general, which is to say the bourgeois and the socialist ones as well as the 'anarchist' ones like Yanovsky, who have all spoken of me as a pogromist against Jews and labeled as anti-Semitic the liberation movement of the Ukrainian peasants and workers of which I was the leader, to detail to me the specific facts instead of blathering vacuously away: just where and just when did I or the aforementioned movement perpetrate such acts?

I had expected that Jews in general would answer my "Appeal" after the manner of people eager to disclose to the civilized world the truth about these blackguards responsible for the massacres of Jews in the Ukraine, or indeed that they might attempt to base their shameful anecdotes about me and the Makhnovist movement upon fairly authentic data in that they involve me in them and peddle them to public opinion.

Thus far, no such evidence advanced by Jews has come to my attention. The only thing that has appeared thus far in the press generally, certain Jewish anarchist organs included, regarding myself and the insurgent movement I led, has been the product of the most shameless lies and of the vulgarity of certain political mavericks and their hirelings. Moreover, revolutionary fighting units made up of Jewish workers played a role of prime importance in that movement. The cowardice of slanderers washes over me, for I have always dismissed it for what it is. Jewish citizens may be assured of this if they note that I said not one single word about the travesty from the pen of one Joseph Kessel, entitled *Makhno and his Jewess*, a novel written on the basis of misinformation regarding myself and the movement connected with me organizationally and theoretically. The nub of that travesty is lifted from the writings of a lick spittle lackey of the Bolsheviks, one Colonel Gerassimenko, recently convicted by the Czech courts of spying on behalf of a Bolshevik military organization.

The novelette is also based upon articles by a bourgeois journalist, one Arbatov, who unashamedly credits me with all manner of violence perpetrated against a troupe of "performing dwarves." An invention from start to finish, of course.

In his novel which simply hives with falsehoods, Kessel contrives to portray me in such an odious light that, at least in those passages where he borrows from the writings of Gerassimenko and Arbatov, he should have named his sources! To the extent that falsehood plays the main role in this novel and that the sources are inconsistent, silence was the only response open to me.

I take a quite different view of the slanders emanating from Jewish societies, which seek to create the impression in their co-religionists that they have diligently scrutinized the despicable and screamingly unjust acts perpetrated against the Jewish population in the Ukraine and whose perpetrators these societies seek to denounce.

A little while ago, one of these societies, which by the way has its headquarters in the kingdom of the Bolsheviks, has issued a book, illustrated with photographs, about the atrocities committed against the Jewish population in the Ukraine and(Belorussia, this on the basis of materials amassed by 'comrade' Ostrovsky, which patently means: of Bolshevik provenance. In this 'historical' document there is nowhere any mention of the anti-Jewish pogroms carried out by the much-vaunted First Red Army Cavalry when it passed through the Ukraine en route from the

Caucasus in May 1920. By contrast, the same document does mention a number of pogroms and alongside prints the photographs of Makhnovist insurgents, though it is not clear what they are doing there, on the one hand, and which, in point of fact are no even Makhnovists, as witness the photograph purporting to show 'Makhnovists on the move' behind a black flag displaying a death's head: this is a photo that has no connection with pogroms and indeed and especially does not show Makhnovists at all.

An even more significant misrepresentation, targeting myself and the Makhnovists alike, can be seen in the photographs showing the streets of Alexandrovsk, allegedly laid waste following a pogrom mounted by Makhnovists, in the summer of 1919. This crude lie is unforgivable in the Jewish society responsible for publication, for it is common knowledge in the Ukraine that at the time in question the Makhnovist insurgent army was far from that region: it had fallen back into the western Ukraine. Indeed, Alexandrovsk had been under Bolshevik control from February to June 1919, and then been in Denikinist hands until the autumn.

With these documents, the Bolshevik-inclined Jewish society has done a great disservice to me and to the Makhnovist movement: unable to find documentary evidence with which to arraign us — for the benefit of its sponsors — on charges of anti-Jewish pogroms, it has resorted to blatant faking of evidence that has no connection either with me or with the insurgent movement. Its perfidious approach is even more glaringly apparent when it reproduces a photograph — "Makhno, a 'peaceable' citizen" when in fact the person shown is someone absolutely unknown to me.

On all these grounds I regarded it as my duty to address myself to the international Jewish community in order to draw attention to the cowardice and lying of certain Jewish associations in thrall to the Bolsheviks, in charging me personally and also the insurgent movement which I led, of anti-Jewish pogroms. International Jewish opinion must scrupulously examine the substance of these infamous allegations, for the peddling of such nonsense is scarcely the best way of establishing, in the eyes of all, the truth about what the Ukraine's Jewish population endured, not forgetting the fact that these lies serve only to misrepresent History completely.

Dyelo Truda No 23-24, April-May 1927, pp. 8-10.

6. THE MAKHNOVSHCHINA AND ANTI-SEMITISM

For the past seven years, almost, the enemies of the Makhnovist revolutionary movement have wallowed in so many lies about it that one might marvel that these people do not take a red face, once in a while at least. It is rather characteristic that these shameless lies directed against myself and the Makhnovist insurgents, indeed against our movement as a whole, can unite folk from very different socio-political camps: among them one can find journalists of every persuasion, writers, scholars and laymen who place obstacles in their path, mavericks and speculators, who occasionally have no hesitation in putting themselves forward as pathfinders for avant-garde revolutionary ideas. One can also come across supposed anarchists, like Yanovsky, from the *Freie Arbeiter Stimme*. All such folk, folk of every persuasion and every hue, have no shame about employing lies against us, without even knowing us, sometimes without any real belief in their own allegations. Such lies are rounded off with innuendo, which consists of forever and always railing at us, without any attempt to verify the grounds for that ranting and raving. In fact, where are the probable grounds to justify this hysteria in the slightest degree? A little while ago, all these bare-faced lies against us Makhnovists, alleging us to have been pogromists, without offering one shred of evidence or any sort of authentication, led me to address the world's Jews through the good offices of the French and Russian libertarian press, to ask them to spell out the sources of all these absurdities, so as to supply specific details regarding pogroms, incitement or instigation of pogroms carried out or launched by the Ukrainian toilers' revolutionary movement led by me.

The well known Parisian 'Faubourg' Club was alone in replying to my "Appeal to the Jews of All Countries." Through the press, the club managers let it be known that, at a meeting on 23 June 1927, the following question would come up for debate: "Was 'General' Makhno the friend of the Jews or did he participate in their slaughter?" It was added that our French comrade Lecoin would be speaking in defense of Makhno.

It goes without saying that as soon as I learned of the holding of this 'Faubourg' debate, I immediately approached the club chairman, Poldes, requesting him by letter that Lecoin be withdrawn and that I be afforded the opportunity to address the club on my own behalf. Following a positive reply, I appeared before the assembled club on 23 June 1927.

However, the particular manner in which debates were conducted in that club and the fact that the matter of concern to me was dealt with only towards the close of the proceedings meant that I was only able to make myself heard very late on, around 11:00 P.M. and I was not able to go into the matter thoroughly. The best I managed was to broach the subject by dealing with the historical nature, sources and patterns of anti-Semitism in the Ukraine.

Perhaps my enemies will make capital out of this factor which was beyond my control and above all of the fact that I was bound hand and foot by it. In fact, according to French police regulations, I was forbidden to communicate with my like-minded French colleagues: as a result, there was no way that I could have organized a public meeting of my own to put my rebuttal of these slanders. Also, some people have brazenly lied and talked about my having been "tried" in Paris. This is a further lie, which has been taken up by my enemies, hypocritical defenders of the rights and independence of the Jewish people who have suffered so much over the past thirty years in Russia and the Ukraine.

Can the facts be squared in any degree at all with these lies? All of the Jewish toilers of the Ukraine, as well as all other Ukrainian toilers are well aware that the movement of which I was for years the leader was a genuine revolutionary workers' movement. At no time did that movement seek to divide the practical organization of the deceived, exploited and oppressed toilers on grounds of race. Quite the opposite: it aimed to unite them into a mighty revolutionary union capable of taking action against their oppressors, especially against the Denikinists who were dyed-in-the-wool anti-Semites. At no time did the movement make it its business to carry out pogroms against Jews nor did it ever encourage any. What is more, the vanguard of the Ukraine's (Makhnovist) revolutionary movement contained many Jewish toilers. The Gulyai-Polye infantry regiment for instance had one company made up exclusively of two hundred Jewish toilers. There was also a four-piece artillery battery, the gunners and defense unit of which were all Jews, commander included. And there were lots of Jewish toilers in the Makhnovist movement who, for personal reasons, preferred to blend in with mixed revolutionary fighting units. These were all free fighters, volunteer enlistments who fought honestly on behalf of the joint endeavors of the toilers. These anonymous fighters had their representatives inside the economic bodies revictualling the entire army. All of which may be verified with the Jewish colonies and villages in the Gulyai-Polye region.

All such Jewish insurgent toilers were under my command for a long period, not for days or months, but rather for entire years. All were witnesses to the manner in which I, the Staff and the entire army conducted ourselves with regard to anti-Semitism and the pogroms that arose from it.

Every attempted pogrom or looting from our side was nipped in the bud. All found guilty of such acts were invariably shot out of hand for their misdeeds. This was the case for instance in May 1919, when some peasant insurgents from Novo-Uspenovka, on leaving the front line for some rest in the rear, came upon two decomposed corpses near a Jewish settlement: assuming these to be the corpses of insurgents murdered by members of the Jewish colony, they vented their spleen on the colony and slaughtered around thirty of its inhabitants. That same day, my Staff dispatched a commission of inquiry to the colony. It discovered the tracks of the perpetrators of the butchery. I immediately sent a special detachment to their village to place them under arrest. Those responsible for the attack on the Jewish colony, namely six individuals, one of them the Bolshevik district commissar, were all shot on 13 May 1919.

The same thing happened in July 1919, when I found myself caught in the crossfire between Denikin and Trotsky — Trotsky was then promising his Party that "it was better that the Ukraine be surrendered to Denikin in its entirety than the possibility of the Makhnovshchina's expanding be allowed to arise" and I was forced to cross over to the right bank of the Dniepr. This was when I met with the famous Grigoriev, the ataman of the Kherson region. Misled by the inane rumors circulating about me and the insurgent movement, Grigoriev sought to conclude an alliance with me and my Staff with an eye to waging a concerted campaign against Denikin and the Bolsheviks.

Talks were opened on the condition, which I required, that, within two weeks, ataman Grigoriev furnish my Staff and the Soviet of the (Makhnovist) Revolutionary Insurgent Army of the Ukraine with documents proving that all reports of pogroms carried out by him on two or three occasions against the Jews of Elizavetgrad were baseless, given that, with time at a premium, I was not able to authenticate them for myself.

That condition gave Grigoriev something to think about: then, as a good soldier and strategist, he consented. To prove to me that he could in no way be a pogromist, he boasted of the fact that his retinue included a Ukrainian representative of the Socialist Revolutionary Party. Then, accusing me of having issued an "Appeal" against him, in the name of my Staff, wherein he had been denounced as an enemy of the revolution, in token of his good faith Grigoriev introduced to me several political representatives who attended him: Nikolai Kopornitsky of the Ukrainian Socialist Revolutionary Party, Seliansky (alias Gorobets) and Koliuzhny of the Ukrainian Social Democratic Party.

This happened at a time when I was on the outskirts of Elizavetgrad with my main combat detachment. I deemed it incumbent upon me as a revolutionary to avail of this opportunity to verify for myself just what the ataman Grigoriev might have done during his occupation of the town. At the same time, some intercepted Denikinist agents revealed to me that, unbeknownst to the toilers of the Kherson region, Grigoriev was preparing to coordinate his movements with the Denikinist headquarters in a build-up to a concerted campaign against the Bolsheviks.

From inhabitants of Elizavetgrad and neighboring villages, as well as from some partisans from Grogoriev's units, I learned that every time he had occupied the town Jews had been massacred. In his presence and on his orders, his partisans had murdered nearly two thousand Jews, including the flower of the Jewish youth: many members of the anarchist, Bolshevik and socialist youth organizations. Some of these had even been taken from prison for slaughter.

Upon learning all this, I promptly declared Grigoriev, the ataman of Kherson — a "Socialist Revolutionary" (sic) — a Denikinist agent and open pogromist, directly culpable for the actions of his supporters against Jews.

At the Sentovo meeting on 27 July 1919, Grigoriev was denounced for what he was and executed on the spot for all to see. That execution and the reasons for it were announced thus: "The pogromist Grigoriev has been executed by Makhnovist leaders: Batko Makhno, Semyon Karetnik and Alexis Chubenko. The Makhnovist movement accepts full responsibility before History for this action." That declaration was endorsed by the members of the Soviet of the Insurgent Army and the Socialist Revolutionary Party members present, including Nikolai Kopornitsky (NOTE: The Social Democrats Seliansky and Koliuzhny had vanished utterly following the execution of Grogoriev.)

That was the sort of treatment I always reserved for those who had carried out pogroms or were in the throes of preparing them. And looters were not spared either, whether from the Insurgent Army's own ranks or outsiders. For example this is what happened in August 1920 when two detachments of Petliurist nationalist leanings, under the command of Levchenko and Matyansha, encircled by us, sent emissaries to us to suggest that they be incorporated into our ranks. The Staff and I received them and agreed that they could be enlisted: however, as soon as we realized that the nationalistic elements from these detachments were engaging in looting and blatant anti-Semitism, we shot them out of hand, in the village of Avereski, in Poltava province. A few days later, their commander Matyansha was also shot for his provocative behavior in the town of Zinkov (Poltava province). His detachment was stripped of its weapons and most of its members cashiered.

In December 1920, there was a repeat of this with Red Army troops, when we successfully withstood the onslaught from Budyenny's cavalry and completely routed the XIth Division of his army, near the village of Petrovo in the Alexandrovsk district, followed by the XIVth Cavalry Division, taking the entire command and Staff prisoners in the latter instance. Many prisoners from the XIth Division expressed an interest in joining the Insurgent Army to combat the autocratic political commissars as they described them. As they were crossing the Kherson region and reached the village of Dobrovelitchka, over half of the population of which was Jewish, certain former Budyennyist or Petliurist cavalrymen, acting on the rumors current in their former units regarding the Makhnovists' hostility towards the "Yids", set about looting the homes of the Jewish villagers. As soon as this came to the attention of experienced Makhnovists, they were all arrested and shot on the spot.

Thus, throughout its entire existence, the Makhnovshchina took an uncompromising line on the anti-Semitism of pogromists: this was because it was a genuinely revolutionary toilers' movement in the Ukraine.

Dyelo Truda No 30-31, November-December 1927, pp. 15-18.

7. In Memory of the Kronstadt Revolt

March 7th is a harrowing date for the toilers of the so-called "Union of Soviet Socialist Republics" who participated in one capacity or another in the events that occurred on that date in Kronstadt. The commemoration of that date is equally painful for the toilers of all countries, for it brings back the memory of what the free workers and sailors of Kronstadt demanded of their Red executioner, the "Russian Communist Party," and its tool, the "Soviet" government, busy doing the Russian revolution to death.

Kronstadt insisted of these statist hangmen that they hand back everything that belonged to the toilers of town and country, given that it was they who had carried out the revolution. The Kronstadters insisted upon the practical implementation of the foundations of the October revolution:

> Freely elected soviets, freedom of speech and freedom of the press for workers and peasants, anarchists and Left Socialist Revolutionaries.

The Russian Communist Party saw this as an unconscionable challenge to its monopolist position in the country and, concealing its craven executioner's face behind the mask of revolutionary and workers' friend, pronounced the free sailors and workers of Kronstadt counter-revolutionaries and then sent against them tens of thousands of obedient cops and slaves: Chekists, Kursanty (Red Army officer cadets — note by Alexandre Skirda), Party members . . . in order to massacre these decent fighters and revolutionaries — the Kronstadters — who had nothing with which to reproach themselves before the revolutionary masses, their only offense having been to feel outrage at the lies and cowardice of the Russian Communist Party which was trampling upon the rights of the toilers and the revolution.

On March 7, 1921, at 6.45 p.m., a storm of artillery fire was unleashed against Kronstadt. As was only natural and inevitable, Kronstadt fought back. Fought back, not just on behalf of their demands, but also on behalf of the other toilers of the country who were struggling from their revolutionary rights, arbitrarily trampled underfoot by the Bolshevik authorities.

Their fight back echoed throughout an enslaved Russia which stood ready to back their just and heroic fight, but was unfortunately powerless to do so, because it had been disarmed, constantly exploited and kept in bondage by the repressive detachments from the Red Army and the Cheka, specially formed to break the free spirit and free will of the country.

It is hard to estimate the losses suffered by the Kronstadt defenders and of the blind mass of the Red Army, but we may rest assured that they numbered upwards of ten thousand dead. For the most part, they were workers and peasants, the very people whom the Party of Lies had used in order to seize power, by gulling them with promises of a better future. It had made use of them for years exclusively in pursuit of its own party interests, so as to spread and entrench its all powerful domination over the country's economic and political life.

Against the Bolshevik oligarchy, Kronstadt defended the very best of the workers' and peasants' struggle in the Russian revolution. For that very reason, the oligarchs exterminated the Kronstadters, some right after the military victory, the remainder in the dungeons and blockhouses inherited from the tsarist and bourgeois regime. Understood thus, the date of March 7th has to appear as a profoundly painful anniversary for the workers of all countries. So it is not just among Russian toilers only that the painful memory of the Kronstadt revolutionaries who perished in the fighting and the survivors who were left to rot in Bolshevik jails should be reawakened on that date. But this matter will not be resolved with moaning: aside from the commemoration of March 7th, the toilers of every land should organize rallies all over the place to protest against the outrages perpetrated in Kronstadt by the Russian Communist Party against revolutionary workers and sailors, and demand the release of the survivors languishing in Bolshevik prisons and interned in the concentration camps in Finland.

Dyelo Truda No. 10, March 1926, pp. 3-4 .

8. THE IDEA OF EQUALITY AND THE BOLSHEVIKS

The 14th Congress of the Russian Communist Party has roundly condemned the notion of equality. Prior to the congress, Zinoviev had mentioned the idea in the course of his polemic against Ustrialov and Bukharin. He declared then that the whole of contemporary philosophy was sustained by the idea of equality. Kalinin spoke up forcefully at the congress against that contention, taking the line that any reference to equality could not help but be harmful and was not to be tolerated. His reasoning was as follows:

'Can we talk to peasants about equality? No, that is out of the question, for in that case, they would set about demanding the same rights as workers, which would be in complete contradiction with the dictatorship of the proletariat. Likewise, can we talk of equality to workers? No, that is out of the question too, for if, say, a communist and a non-party member do the same job, the difference resides in the former being paid twice the wage of the latter. To concede equality would allow non-party members to demand the same pay as is paid out to a communist. Is that acceptable, comrades? No, it is not. Can we call for equality among communists then? No, that is not on either, for they too occupy different positions, in terms of their rights and their material circumstances alike.'

On the basis of such considerations, Kalinin concluded that Zinoviev's use of the term "equality" could only have been demagogic and harmful. In his reply, Zinoviev in turn told the congress that, whilst he had spoken of equality, he had meant it in quite a different sense. As for himself, all he had had in mind was "socialist equality," that is, the equality that would one day come to pass in a more or less distant future. For the time being, until such time as the world revolution had taken place and as there was no way of knowing when it would, there could be no question of any equality. In particular, there could be no equality of rights, for that would risk dragging us in the direction of very dangerous "democratic" deviations.

This understanding on the notion of equality was not spelled out in a resolution from the congress. But, essentially, the two camps that clashed at the congress were agreed in regarding the idea of equality as intolerable.

Formerly, and not all that long ago, the Bolsheviks spoke quite a different language. It was under the banner of equality that they operated during the great Russian revolution, to overthrow the bourgeoisie, in concert with the workers and peasants, at whose expense they rose to political control over the country. It was under those colors that, after eight years of ruling over the lives and liberties of the toilers of the former Russia — henceforth to be known as the 'Union of Soviet Socialist Republics' the Bolshevik tsars sought to persuade the toilers of that 'Union,' (oppressed by them), as well as the toilers from other countries (which they do not yet control), that if they have persecuted, left to rot in prison or deported and murdered their political enemies, this has been done exclusively in the name of the revolution, its egalitarian foundations (which they allegedly had introduced into the revolution) which their enemies supposedly wished to destroy.

It shall soon be eight years since the blood of anarchists began to flow because of their refusal to servilely bow before the violence or effrontery of those who have seized power, nor before their famously lying ideology and their utter irresponsibility.

In that criminal act, an act that cannot be described as other than a bloodlust of the Bolshevik gods, the finest offspring of the revolution have perished because they were the most loyal exponents of revolutionary ideals and because they could not be bribed into betraying them. In honestly defending the precepts of the revolution, these children of the revolution sought to fend off the madness of the Bolshevik gods and find a way out of their dead end, so as to forge a path to real freedom and genuine equality of the toilers.

The Bolshevik potentates quickly realized that the aspirations of these children of the revolution would spell doom for their madness and above all for the privileges they adroitly inherited from the toppled bourgeoisie, then treacherously beefed up to their advantage. On these grounds they condemned the revolutionaries to death. Men with the souls of slaves supported them in this and the blood flowed. For the past eight years it has gone on flowing, and in the name of what, we might ask? In the name of freedom and equality of the toilers, say the Bolsheviks, continuing to exterminate thousands of nameless revolutionaries, fighters for the social revolution, labeled as "bandits" and "counter-revolutionaries."

With that shameless falsehood, the Bolsheviks have hidden the true state of affairs in Russia from the eyes of toilers the world over, particularly their utter bankruptcy in the matter of building socialism, when this is all too apparent to all who have the eyes to see.

Anarchists alerted toilers of every country in time to the Bolsheviks' crimes in the Russian revolution. Bolshevism, embodying the ideal of a centralizing State, has shown itself as the deadly enemy of the free spirit of revolutionary toilers. Resorting to unprecedented measures, it has sabotaged the development of the revolution and besmirched the honor of its finest aspect. Successfully disguised, it concealed its real face from the gaze of the toilers, passing itself off as the champion of their interests. Only now, after an eight years' reign, increasingly flirting with the international bourgeoisie, does it begin to cast aside its mask of revolution and expose to the world of labor the face of a rapacious exploiter.

The Bolsheviks have jettisoned the idea of equality, not just in practice but also in theory, for the very enunciation of it strikes them as dangerous now. This is quite understandable, for their entire rule depends on a diametrically contrasting notion, on a screaming inequality, the entire horror and evils of which have battened upon the backs of the workers. Let us hope that the toilers of every country may draw the necessary conclusions and, in turn, finish with the Bolsheviks, those exponents of the idea of slavery and oppressors of Labor.

Dyelo Truda No. 9, February 1926, pp. 9-10.

9. The Paths of "Proletarian" Power

It is a long time now since the avant-garde socialist intelligentsia framed, in more or less rounded form, the aims of the historical struggle of the proletariat against the bourgeoisie and since proletarians, swallowing that formulation by the intelligentsia whole, entered the lists of that struggle under the intelligentsia's leadership. There is no denying that this was a triumph for the intelligentsia which has thus set itself the target of leading the proletariat on to complete emancipation, by means of the destruction of bourgeois power and the bourgeois State, which are to be supplanted by a "proletarian" State and power.

Very naturally, neither the intelligentsia nor the proletariat itself has been stinting in its efforts and investigations designed to expose to the widest possible audience all the harm done by the bourgeois State. Thanks to which, they have been able to nurse and develop among the toiling masses the notion of a "proletarian" power that would supposedly resolve all their problems. According to this view, the proletariat, through its class power and State, would make use of the only existing means whereby it and other classes might free themselves of the bourgeoisie and introduce the principles of freedom and egalitarianism into the relations between people. Such a forecast of the destiny of "proletarian" power has always struck us anarchists as a crass error. In times gone by, our comrades constantly revolted against this notion and also demonstrated where the statists had gone wrong in differentiating between "proletarian" power and the State in general and in ascribing to the former a mission that was profoundly alien to it.

Statist socialists, however, remained true to their authoritarian tradition and it was armed with that outlook that they seized upon the Great Russian Revolution, a revolution of a depth and breadth in social implications for which History had seen no equal. As for us anarchists, we opposed their mistaken forecast about the destiny of "proletarian" power. In the course of the polemic between us, we showed the statists that any State, whether bourgeois or proletarian, tends, by its very nature, simply to exploit and oppress man, to destroy in each and every one of us all the natural qualities of the human spirit that strive for equality and for the solidarity that underpins it. Which earned us only greater hatred from the statist socialists. Now, the existence and practice of "proletarian" power in Russia have borne out and bear out the accuracy of our analysis. The "proletarian" State has increasingly betrayed its true nature and proved that its proletarian-ness was a mere figment, as proletarians have been able to appreciate since the early years of the revolution, the more so since they themselves helped install it. The fact that in the course of its degeneration the "proletarian" power has showed itself to be nothing more than a State power pure and simple is now beyond dispute and has induced it to desist from artful concealment of its real face. Its practice had abundantly proved that its goals and those of the Great Russian Revolution had absolutely nothing in common. Over all those years of hypocrisy, it has failed to subordinate the aims of the Russian Revolution to its own ends peaceably, and has had to confront all who threatened to expose its true essence — as a huge and festering ulcer upon the body of the revolution — the cowardice and treachery of which spell death and ruination to all without exception, and primarily to those who try to be independent and operate freely. One might ask oneself: how did all of this come to pass? According to Marx and Lenin, "proletarian" power ought not to bear any resemblance at all to bourgeois power. Does not some segment of the vanguard of the proletariat bear a share of the blame for this state of affairs?

Many anarchists tend to reckon that the proletariat counts for nothing in this, having been, so to speak, duped by the caste of socialist intellectuals, who supposedly aspire, over a series of purely sociohistorical phenomena and by reason of the logic of inevitable amendments to the State, to replace the power of the bourgeoisie with their own power. It is supposedly on these grounds that the socialist intelligentsia would seek, on a permanent basis, to direct the struggle of the proletariat against the capitalist, bourgeois world.

As I see it, such an argument is neither quite accurate nor is it really adequate. Russia's revolutionary experience supplies us with objective data galore in this connection. It shows us beyond rebuttal that the proletariat was not at all homogeneous during the revolution. Thus, the urban proletariat, whenever it participated in the overthrow of the power of the class enemy — the bourgeoisie — in many towns, hesitated for a moment between the paths of the revolutions of February and October 1917. It was only after a time, after October's military victory over February, that a significant fraction of the urban proletariat began to throw in its lot with the part of its brothers, the direct architects of the gains of October. Soon, that segment of the proletariat not only forgot to defend those gains for itself, but also was in more of a hurry to go over to the Bolshevik party on power, which was cute enough to flatter it immoderately, cultivating in it a certain taste for class privileges, political, economic and juridical. Drinking deeply of these class privileges, this segment of the proletariat fell equally in love with its "proletarian class State." Self-evidently, the Bolshevik social democratic party wholly supported and encouraged it in this trend, for it offered the party great scope for implementation of its own program, which consisted of utilizing the practical struggle of the proletariat so as to bring the bulk of the proletariat to heel and then take over State power in its name. Along the way, the better to stand out from the crowd, the Bolshevik social democratic party turned itself into the "Bolshevik Communist" party, unashamedly resorting to the most brazen demagogy and shrinking from no ploy, not hesitating, as the need arose, to cannibalize the programs of other political groupings: all for the sole purpose of binding the proletariat (to which it pledged its unstinting help, when in fact it was pursuing its own ends alone) all the better to itself. In this sense, the party was the finest embodiment of the historical ambitions of the intellectual caste: supplanting the bourgeoisie in power and exercising that power, no matter the cost. A sizable segment of the proletariat failed to stand up to its views: indeed, quite the opposite, it identified with what it did and became its accomplice.

That segment of the proletariat had, however, been educated over generations to the notion that the proletariat would only emancipate itself from the bourgeoisie when it managed to break its power and destroy its state organization in order to clear the way for the construction of its own. Nevertheless, this fraction of the proletariat helped the Bolshevik-Communist party to organize its "proletarian power" and erect "its" class State.

The path taken and the means employed did not take long to assimilate that fraction of the proletariat in every particular to the overthrown bourgeoisie, rendering it every whit as impudent and arrogant, with no scruples about using the most savage violence to enforce its domination over the people and the revolution.

It goes without saying that this violence was second nature to the party's intellectual caste, for it had been schooling itself in its use for many a long year and had become intoxicated with it. As for the bulk of the proletariat — yesterday's mute slave — the violence deployed against its fellows is wholly alien to it. Busy with the building of its "class State," part of the proletariat was thus induced to behave, through the use of violence, in a repugnant fashion with regard to the individual liberty, freedom of speech and expression of any revolutionary organization, the moment that the latter impudently took issue with "proletarian power." That fraction of the proletariat scurried to ensconce themselves, under the leadership of the Bolshevik-Communist party, in the positions left vacant by the despots of the toppled bourgeoisie, becoming in their turn a tyrannical master-class, showing no hesitation, in pursuit of these ends, about using the ghastliest violence indiscriminately against all who opposed its designs. At the same time, this behavior was artfully concealed behind the "defense of the revolution."

Such violence was employed above all against the body of the Russian revolution, for the exclusive benefit of the narrow interests of one fraction of the proletariat and of the Bolshevik-Communist party, and on behalf of their complete domination of all the other laboring classes. This cannot be regarded simply as the proletariat blown temporarily off course. Yet again, we can see very clearly how all State power brazenly shows what it is made of, with the adjective "proletarian" changing absolutely nothing.

As I see it, it is for all these reasons that all foreign comrades who have not had this first-hand experience, should carefully scrutinize all the stages of the Russian revolution, particularly the role played in it by the Bolshevik-Communist party and by that fraction of the proletariat that has followed it. This so that they may steer clear of the same errors, in the light of the shameless demagogy of the Bolsheviks and their supporters, regarding the serviceability of "proletarian power."

It is equally true that the campaign currently being waged by all our comrades against Bolshevik lies should be deployed in support of reliable information concerning anything they might themselves put to the broad masses in replacement of this "proletarian power." Fine slogans are not enough, although the masses are often not indifferent to them. This struggle is waged on the basis of concrete situations and continually leads to the posing of crucial and urgent questions: how and by which methods of social action should the toiling masses seek their complete emancipation?

Such questions should be answered as directly as possible and with the utmost clarity. That is a vital necessity, not only if an active struggle is to be conducted against the capitalist and bourgeois world, but also for our anarchist movement, for the influence of our ideas upon the launch and the outcome of that struggle hinges upon it. Which means that the proletariat must not repeat the mistake made by its brethren in Russia, which is to say, must not busy itself with the organizing of a "proletarian power" under the baton of any party, even should it label itself "proletarian," but only with seeing to the satisfaction of everyone's needs and defending the revolution against all manner of State authorities.

Probuzdeniye No. 18, January 1932, pp. 45-48.

10."Soviet" Power —
Its Present and Its Future

Many people, especially left-wing politicians, have a tendency to regard "soviet" power as a State power different from all the rest, to be sure, but painting that difference in the rosiest of hues:

> "Soviet power," they tell us, "is a worker and peasant power and, as such, has a great future ahead of it."

There can be no more absurd assertion. "Soviet" power is a power no better and no worse than any other. Currently, it is every bit as wobbly and absurd as any State power in general. In certain respects, it is even more absurd than the rest. Having achieved total political domination over the country, it has become the unchallenged master of its economic resources and, not content with that crassly exploitative situation, it has sensed, welling up from within itself, the deceptive sentiment of a spiritual "perfection," a sentiment that it seeks to peddle to the country's toiling revolutionary people. This has left its proletarian "spirit" less revolutionary, but more impudent. Thus, it seeks to foist itself upon the bamboozled populace as its spiritual master: in this, it is faithful to the boundless and irresponsible effrontery of every State power. It is an open secret that this supposed "perfection" of the regime is merely the perfection of its mentor, the Bolshevik-Communist party. All of which is nothing more than a bare-faced lie, abject duplicity and criminal impudence towards the toiling masses, in whose name and thanks to whom the great Russian revolution, currently flayed by the authorities to the benefit of their party privileges and those of the proletarian minority which, under the party's sway, believed it could identify with the labels of "proletarian" State and the dictatorship of the "proletariat," so seductive to those who know no better, was carried out. A minority that nonetheless lets itself be dragged along by the bridle by that party, in silence, without having any say in the matter, bereft of the right to be briefed in detail about what was treacherously concocted and accomplished yesterday, and what is still being cooked up today against its proletarian brethren, the ones that refuse to be a blind, unspeaking cat's paw and who do not swallow the lies of the party that wears a proletarian disguise.

In spite of everything, one might wonder if such conduct by the Bolshevik authorities with regard to the toilers may show itself differently in the realm of their "spiritual" education. It strikes me that that cannot but be the case. As evidence of that I would cite the persistence of revolutionary consciousness in the toilers of the USSR, a source of grave disquiet to the regime, and the fact that the Bolshevik party seeks to replace it with a political consciousness manufactured after the pattern of its program.

This is the factor that explains why Bolshevik authorities are facing more and more difficulties and why they stupidly seek to round off their economic and political despotism with a spiritual grip upon the laboring people. It goes without saying that the regime's current straits closely determine its future prospects: a future that is fraught with uncertainty, for want of a plainly favorable present. In fact, the present position is so visibly unfavorable for millions of workers that we may expect, any year now, bloody insurrections and revolutions erupting against the Bolshevik-Communist order. It is very obvious that the insurrectionist and revolutionary spirit of the USSR's workers should enjoy the support of any and every revolutionary. However, counter-revolutionaries and the enemies of the toilers must not make capital out of that support. Consequently, that support should have no aim other than the destruction of the present senseless and irresponsible order, set up for the benefit of the privileges of party members and their hirelings.

The lunacy of this regime must be eliminated and replaced by the vital principles of the exploited workers, on a basis of solidarity, freedom and equal voice for each and every person, in short, for all concerned with genuine emancipation. This is a matter that concerns all Russian revolutionaries: all who find themselves exiles or inside the USSR must, as I see it, concern themselves with it first of all: as well as all proletarians and intellectuals of revolutionary disposition: to whom I would add all opponents of, and political fugitives from the Bolshevik regime, provided that it be for truly revolutionary considerations.

That is how I see the present and the future of "soviet power," as well as the stance that Russian revolutionaries of all persuasions must adopt with regard to it. In my view, revolutionaries cannot pose the problem differently. They must appreciate that, if Bolshevik power is to be fought, one has to be able to boast in the greatest measure the values that it used and enunciated in order to seize power: values that it still professes, moreover, to champion, albeit without sincerity.

Otherwise, the struggle of revolutionaries would turn out to be, if not counter-revolutionary, then at least of no use to the cause of millions of toilers gulled, oppressed and exploited by the Bolshevik-Communists, toilers that a revolutionary should be helping, whatever the cost, to break free of the vicious circle of falsehood and oppression.

Bor'ba (The Struggle) Paris, No. 19-20, 25 October 1931, W- 2-3

(This paper was published by a number of anti-Stalinist and anti-Trotskyist Soviet defectors, who distanced themselves from the Bolshevik regime on a basis of reversion to the power of the free soviets of 1917 and the demands of the Kronstadt rebels of 1921. The leading light behind the magazine was Gregory Bessedovsky, a Ukrainian former soviet diplomat who quit the USSR's Paris embassy sensationally and devoted himself to violent denunciation of the corruption of the Stalinist regime. See his book *Oui, J'accuse!* Paris, 1930 — Note by Alexandre Skirda)

11. The Struggle Against the State

The fact that the modern State is the organizational form of an authority founded upon arbitrariness and violence in the social life of toilers is independent of whether it may be "bourgeois" or "proletarian." It relies upon oppressive centralism, arising out of the direct violence of a minority deployed against the majority. In order to enforce and impose the legality of its system, the State resorts not only to the gun and money, but also to potent weapons of psychological pressure. With the aide of such weapons, a tiny group of politicians enforces psychological repression of an entire society, and, in particular, of the toiling masses, conditioning them in such a way as to divert their attention from the slavery instituted by the State.

So it must be clear that if we are to combat the organized violence of the modern State, we have to deploy powerful weapons, appropriate to the magnitude of the task.

Thus far, the methods of social action employed by the revolutionary working class against the power of the oppressors and exploiters — the State and Capital — in conformity with libertarian ideas, were insufficient to lead the toilers on to complete victory.

It has come to pass in History that the workers have defeated Capital, but the victory then slipped from their grasp, because some State power emerged, amalgamating the interests of private capital and those of State capitalism for the sake of success over the toilers.

The experience of the Russian revolution has blatantly exposed our shortcomings in this regard. We must not forget that, but should rather apply ourselves to identifying those shortcomings plainly.

We may acknowledge that our struggle against the State in the Russian revolution was remarkable, despite the disorganization by which our ranks were afflicted: remarkable above all insofar as the destruction of that odious institution is concerned.

But, by contrast, our struggle was insignificant in the realm of construction of the free society of toilers and its social structures, which might have ensure that it prospered beyond reach of the tutelage of the State and its repressive institutions.

The fact that we libertarian communists or anarcho-syndicalists failed to anticipate the sequel to the Russian revolution and that we failed to make haste to devise new forms of social activity in time, led many of our groups and organizations to dither yet again in their political and socio-strategic policy on the fighting front of the Revolution.

If we are to avert a future relapse into these same errors, when a revolutionary situation comes about, and in order to retain the cohesion and coherence of our organizational line, we must first of all amalgamate all of our forces into one active collective, then without further ado, define our constructive conception of economic, social, local and territorial units, so that they are outlined in detail (free soviets), and in particular describe in broad outline their basic revolutionary mission in the struggle against the State. Contemporary life and the Russian revolution require that.

Those who have blended in with the very ranks of the worker and peasant masses, participating actively in the victories and defeats of their campaign, must without doubt come to our own conclusions, and more specifically to an appreciation that our struggle against the State must be carried on until the State has been utterly eradicated: they will also acknowledge that the toughest role in that struggle is the role of the revolutionary armed force.

It is essential that the action of the Revolution's armed forces be linked with the social and economic unit, wherein the laboring people will organize itself from the earliest days of the revolution onwards, so that total self-organization of life may be introduced, out of reach of all statist structures.

From this moment forth, anarchists must focus their attention upon that aspect of the Revolution. They have to be convinced that, if the revolution's armed forces are organized into huge armies or into lots of local armed detachments, they cannot but overcome the State's incumbents and defenders, and thereby bring about the conditions needed by the toiling populace supporting the revolution, so that it may cut all ties with the past and look to the final detail of the process of constructing a new socioeconomic existence.

The State will, though, be able to cling to a few local enclaves and try to place multifarious obstacles in the path of the toilers' new life, slowing the pace of growth and harmonious development of new relationships founded on the complete emancipation of man.

The final and utter liquidation of the State can only come to pass when the struggle of the toilers is oriented along the most libertarian lines possible, when the toilers will themselves determine the structures of their social action. These structures should assume the form of organs of social and economic self-direction, the form of free "anti-authoritarian" soviets. The revolutionary workers and their vanguard — the anarchists — must analyze the nature and structure of these soviets and specify their revolutionary functions in advance. It is upon that, chiefly, that the positive evolution and development of anarchist ideas in the ranks of those who will accomplish the liquidation of the State on their own account in order to build a free society, will be dependent.

Dyelo Truda No.17, October 1926, pp. 5-6

12. THE FIRST OF MAY: SYMBOL OF A NEW ERA IN THE LIFE AND STRUGGLE OF THE TOILERS

In the socialist world, the first of May is considered the Labor holiday. This is a mistaken description that has so penetrated the lives of the toilers that in many countries that day is indeed celebrated as such. In fact, the first of May is not at all a holiday for the toilers. No, the toilers should not stay in their workshops or in the fields on that date. On that date, toilers all over the world should come together in every village, every town, and organize mass rallies, not to mark that date as statist socialists and especially the Bolsheviks conceive it, but rather to gauge the measure of their strength and assess the possibilities for direct armed struggle against a rotten, cowardly, slaveholding order rooted in violence and falsehood. It is easiest for all the toilers to come together on that historic date, already part of the calendar, and most convenient for them to express their collective will, as well as enter into common discussion of everything related to essential matters of the present and the future.

Over forty years ago, the American workers of Chicago and its environs assembled on the first of May. There they listened to addresses from many socialist orators, and more especially those from anarchist orators, for they fairly gobbled up libertarian ideas and openly sided with the anarchists.

That day those American workers attempted, by organizing themselves, to give expression to their protest against the iniquitous order of the State and Capital of the propertied. That was what the American libertarians Spies, Parsons and others spoke about. It was at this point that this protest rally was interrupted by provocations by the hirelings of Capital and it ended with the massacre of unarmed workers, followed by the arrest and murder of Spies, Parsons and other comrades.

The workers of Chicago and district had not assembled to celebrate the May Day holiday. They had gathered to resolve, in common, the problems of their lives and their struggles.

Today too, wheresoever the toilers have freed themselves from the tutelage of the bourgeoisie and the social democracy linked to it (Menshevik or Bolshevik, it makes no difference) or even try to do so, they regard the first of May as the occasion of a get-together when they will concern themselves with their own affairs and consider the matter of their emancipation. Through these aspirations, they give expression to their solidarity with and regard for the memory of the Chicago martyrs. Thus they sense that the first of May cannot be a holiday for them. So, despite the claims of "professional socialists," tending to portray it as the Feast of Labor, the first of May can be nothing of the sort for conscious workers.

The first of May is the symbol of a new era in the life and struggle of the toilers, an era that each year offers the toilers fresh, increasingly tough and decisive battles against the bourgeoisie, for the freedom and independence wrested from them, for their social ideal.

Dyelo Truda No.36, 1928, p. 2-3.

13. ANARCHISM AND OUR TIMES

Anarchism is not merely a doctrine that treats of man's social life, in the narrow meaning with which the term is invested in political dictionaries, and sometimes, at meetings, by our propagandist speakers. It is also a teaching that embraces the whole existence of man as a rounded individual.

Over the course of the elaboration of its overall world picture, anarchism has set itself a very specific task: to encompass the world in its entirety, sweeping aside all manner of obstacles, present and yet to come, which might be posed by bourgeois capitalist science and technology. This with the aim of supplying man with the most exhaustive possible explanation of existence in this world and of making the best possible fist of all the problems which may confront it: this approach should help it to internalize a *consciousness* of the anarchism naturally inherent in it — that, at least, is what I suppose — to the extent that it is continually being faced with partial manifestations thereof.

It is on the basis of the will of the individual that the libertarian teaching can be embodied in real life and clear a path that will help man to banish all spirit of submission from his bosom.

When it develops, anarchism knows no bounds. It acknowledges no banks within which it might be confined and fixed. Just like human existence, it has no definitive formulas for its aspirations and objectives.

As I see it, the right that every man enjoys to total freedom, as defined by the theoretical postulates of anarchism, could only be, for him, a means through which to achieve more or less complete blossoming, whilst continuing to develop. Having banished from man that spirit of submission that has been artificially thrust upon him, anarchism thereafter becomes the keynote idea of human society on its march towards the attainment of all its goals.

In our times, anarchism is still regarded as *theoretically* weak: furthermore, some argue that it is often interpreted wrongly. However, its exponents have plenty to say about it: many are constantly prattling about it, militating actively and sometimes complaining of its lack of success (I imagine, in this last instance, that this attitude is prompted by the failure to devise, through research, the social wherewithal vital to anarchism if it is to gain a foothold in contemporary society) . . .

Each and every one of us is agreed that cohesion between all active anarchists, in the form of a serious collective activity, is what is needed. It would, therefore, be very surprising for opponents of that Union in our ranks to declare themselves. The issue to be resolved relates only to the organizational format that such a Union of anarchists might assume.

Personally, I am inclined to accept as the most appropriate and most necessary organizational format the one that would offer itself as *a Union of anarchists constructed on the basis of the principles of collective discipline and concerted direction of all anarchist forces.* Thus, all organizations affiliating to it would be inter-connected not just by a community of socio-revolutionary goals, but also by a common subscription to the means that would lead us there.

The activities of local organizations can be adapted, as far as possible, to suit local conditions: however, such activities must, unfailingly, be consonant with the pattern of the overall organizational practice of the Union of anarchists covering the whole country.

The Struggle Against the State and Other Essays

Whether this Union describes itself as a party or as something else is a matter of merely secondary importance. The essential point is that it should focus all anarchist forces upon uniform and common practice against the enemy, pressing ahead with the struggle for toilers' rights, implementation of the social revolution and the installation of the anarchist society!

Dyelo Truda No. 6, November 1925, pp. 6-7.

14. OUR ORGANIZATION

The times through which the working class world-wide is presently passing requires that revolutionary anarchists strain their imaginations and their energies to the fullest if they are to clarify the most important issues.

Those of our comrades who played an active part in the Russian revolution and who have kept faith with their convictions will be sensible of the harmfulness that absence of solid organization has brought to our movement. Those comrades are well-placed to render particular service to the quest for union currently being conducted. It has not gone unnoticed by those comrades, I imagine, that anarchism was a factor for insurrection among the toiling revolutionary masses in Russia and in the Ukraine: it incited them to join in the struggle everywhere. However, the absence of a great specifically anarchist organization, capable of marshaling its resources against the revolution's enemies, left it powerless to assume any organizational role. The libertarian thrust in the revolution has suffered the dire consequences of that.

If they have grasped that shortcoming, the Russian and Ukrainian anarchists should not permit a repetition of this phenomenon. The lesson of the past is too painful and, bearing that in mind, they ought to be the first to teach by example through the cohesiveness of their forces. How? By setting up an organization that can accomplish anarchism's missions, not just when the social revolution is being hatched, but also in its wake. Such an organization should unite all of anarchism's revolutionary forces and unhesitatingly set about preparing the masses for the social revolution and the struggle to achieve the anarchist society.

Although the majority of us are alive to the necessity of such an organization, it is regrettable that we have to record that there is only a tiny number prepared to tackle it with the commitment and consistency that are indispensable.

At the moment, events are gathering pace throughout Europe as a whole and that includes Russia, enmeshed though she may be in the nets of the Pan-Bolsheviks. The day is not far off when we will again be called upon to take an active part in these events. If we answer the call again without first having equipped ourselves with an adequate organization, we will still be powerless to preclude events from being sucked into the vortex of statist systems.

Wheresoever human life is to be found, anarchism assumes a concrete existence. On the other hand, it becomes accessible to the individual only where it boasts propagandists and militants, who have honestly and entirely severed their connections with the slave mentality of our age, something, by the way, that brings savage persecution down upon their heads. Such militants aspire to serve their beliefs with disinterest, without fearing to uncover unsuspected aspects in the course of their development, the better to digest them as they proceed, if need be, and in this way they labor for the success of the anarchist spirit over the spirit of submission. Two theses arise out of the above:

- the first is that anarchism assumes multifarious expressions and forms, whilst retaining a perfect integrity in its essentials.

- the second is that it is inherently revolutionary and can adopt only revolutionary modes of struggle against its enemies.

In the course of its revolutionary struggle, anarchism not merely overthrows governments and discards their laws, but also sets about the society that spawned their values, their "mores" and their "morality," which is what makes it increasingly comprehensible and digestible to the oppressed portion of mankind.

All of which inclines us to the firm belief that anarchism can no longer remain walled up inside the narrow parameters of a marginal thinking to which only a few tiny groups operating in isolation subscribe. Its natural influence upon the mentality of struggling human groups is all too apparent. If that influence is to be assimilated in a conscious fashion, it must henceforth equip itself with new approaches and start here and now to borrow the approach of social practices.

Dyelo Truda No. 4, September 1925, pp. 7-8.

15. On Revolutionary Discipline

Some comrades have put the following question to me: How do I conceive revolutionary discipline? Let me answer that.

I take revolutionary discipline to mean the self-discipline of the individual, set in the context of a strictly prescribed collective activity equally incumbent upon all.

This should be the responsible policy line of the members of that collective, leading to strict congruence between its practice and its theory.

Without discipline inside the organization, there is no way of undertaking any consequential revolutionary activity at all. In the absence of discipline, the revolutionary vanguard cannot exist, for in that case it would find itself in utter disarray in its practice and would be incapable of identifying the tasks of the moment or of living up to the initiator role that the masses expect of it.

I envisage this question against the backdrop of observation and experience of consistent revolutionary practice. For my part, I take as my basis the experience of the Russian revolution, which bore within it a content that was essentially libertarian in many respects.

Had anarchists been closely connected in organizational terms and had they in their actions abided strictly by a well-defined discipline, they would never have suffered such a rout. But, because the anarchists "of all persuasions and tendencies" did not represent (not even in their specific groups) a homogeneous collective with a well-defined policy of action, for that very reason, these anarchists were unable to withstand the political and strategic scrutiny which revolutionary circumstances imposed upon them. Disorganization reduced them to political impotence, separating them into two categories: the first made up of those who hurled themselves into systematic occupation of bourgeois properties, where they set up house and lived in comfort. These are the ones I term "tourists," the various anarchists who beetled around from town to town, in hope of stumbling across a place to live for a time along the way, taking their leisure and hanging around as long as possible to live in comfort and ease.

The other category was made up of those who severed all real connections with anarchism (although a few of them inside the USSR are now passing themselves off as the sole representatives of revolutionary anarchism) and fairly swooped upon the positions offered them by the Bolsheviks, even when the authorities were shooting anarchists who remained true to their revolutionary credentials by denouncing the Bolsheviks' treachery.

In the light of these facts, it will be readily understood why I cannot remain indifferent to the nonchalance and negligence currently to be encountered in our circles.

For one thing, it prevents the establishment of a coherent libertarian collective that would allow anarchists to assume their rightful place in the revolution, and, for another, it leads to a situation where we make do with fine words and grand ideas, whilst fading away when the time for action comes.

That is why I am speaking about a libertarian organization that rests upon the principle of fraternal discipline. Such an organization would lead to the crucial understanding between all of the living forces of revolutionary anarchism and would assist it in taking its rightful place in the struggle of Labor against Capital.

In this fashion, libertarian ideas can only gain a mass following, and not be impoverished. Only empty-headed, irresponsible chatter-boxes could balk at such an organizational set-up.

Organizational responsibility and discipline should not be controversial: they are the traveling companions of the practice of social anarchism.

Dyelo Truda No. 7-8, December 1925-January 1926, p.6.

16. THE ABC OF THE REVOLUTIONARY ANARCHIST

Anarchism means man living free and working constructively. It means the destruction of everything that is directed against man's natural, healthy aspirations.

Anarchism is not exclusively a theoretical teaching emanating from programs artificially conceived with an eye to the regulation of life: it is a teaching derived from life across all its wholesome manifestations, skipping over all artificial criteria.

The social and political visage of anarchism is a free, anti-authoritarian society, one that enshrines freedom, equality and solidarity between all its members.

In anarchism, Right means the responsibility of the individual, the sort of responsibility that brings with it an authentic guarantee of freedom and social justice for each and for all, in all places and at all times. It is out of this that communism springs.

Anarchism is naturally innate in man: communism is the logical extrapolation from it.

These assertions require theoretical support in the shape of assistance from scientific analysis and concrete facts, so that they may become fundamental postulates of anarchism. However, the great libertarian theorists, like Godwin, Proudhon, Bakunin, Johann Most, Kropotkin, Malatesta, Sébastien Faure and lots of others were, I suppose at any rate, loath to confine their doctrine within rigid, definitive parameters. Quite the opposite. It might be said that anarchism's scientific dogma is the aspiration to demonstrate that it is inherent in human nature never to rest on its laurels. The only thing that is unchanging in scientific anarchism is its natural tendency to reject all fetters and any attempt by man to exploit his fellow men. In place of the fetters of the slavery currently extant in human society which, by the way, socialism has not done away with, nor can it — anarchism plants freedom and man's inalienable right to make use of that freedom.

As a revolutionary anarchist, I shared the life of the Ukrainian people during the revolution. Throughout its activity, that people instinctively felt the vital attraction of libertarian ideas and, equally, paid the tragic price for that. Without yielding, I tasted the same dramatic rigors of that collective struggle but, very often, I found myself powerless to comprehend and then to articulate the demands of the moment. Generally speaking, I quickly came to my senses and I clearly grasped that the goal for which I and my comrades were calling for struggle was readily assimilated by the masses fighting for the freedom and independence of the individual and of mankind as a whole.

Experience of practical struggle strengthened my conviction that anarchism educates man in a living way. It is a teaching every bit as revolutionary as life, and it is as varied and potent in its manifestations as man's creative existence and, indeed, is intimately bound up with that.

As a revolutionary anarchist, and for as long as I retain even the most tenuous connection with that label, I will summon you, my humiliated brother, to the struggle to make a reality of the anarchist ideal. In fact, it is only through that struggle for freedom, equality and solidarity that you will reach an understanding of anarchism.

So, anarchism is present in man naturally: historically, it liberates him from the (artificially acquired) slave mentality and helps him become a conscious fighter against slavery in all its guises. It is in that regard that anarchism is revolutionary.

The more a man becomes aware, through reflection, of his servile condition, the more indignant he becomes, the more the anarchist spirit of freedom, determination and action waxes inside him. That is true of every individual, man or woman, even though they may never have heard of the word "anarchism" before.

The nature of man is anarchist: it kicks against anything tending to make it a prisoner. As I see it, this, man's natural essence, is well expressed by the scientific term anarchism. The latter, as an ideal of life in men, plays a meaningful role in human evolution. The oppressors as much as the oppressed, begin, little by little, to come alive to that role: so the former aspire by hook or by crook to misrepresent that ideal, whilst the latter aspire to make it the easier to attain.

Comprehension of the anarchist ideal grows in slave and master alike as modern civilization grows.

Despite the ends to which the latter has thus far been turned — lulling and thwarting every natural tendency in man to protest every trespass against his dignity — it has not been able to silence independent scientific minds which have exposed the true provenance of man and demonstrated the nonexistence of God, hitherto considered the Creator of Mankind. Thereafter, it has naturally become easier to offer irrefutable proof of the artificial nature of "divine ordinances" on earth and of the ignominious relations that they establish between men.

All of these happenings have been of considerable assistance to the conscious development of anarchist ideas. Equally it is true that artificial notions have come to light at the same time: liberalism and that allegedly "scientific" socialism, one of the branches of which is represented by Bolshevism-Communism. However, despite all their vast influence upon the psychology of modern society, or at any rate upon a large part thereof, and despite their victory over the classical reaction on the one hand, and over the individual personality on the other, these artificial notions tend to slip down the slope leading to the familiar forms of the old world.

The free man, who achieves consciousness and expresses it around himself, inevitably lays to rest and always will lay to rest, the whole of mankind's ignoble past, as well as all that that implied in terms of deceit, arbitrary violence and degradation. It will also lay these artificial teachings to rest.

From this moment forth, the individual little by little struggles free of the carapace of lies and cowardice in which the earthly gods have wrapped him since birth, and that with the aid of the brute force of bayonet, ruble, "justice" and hypocritical science — the science of the sorcerers' apprentices.

In sloughing off such infamy, the individual attains a completeness that opens his eyes to the map of the world: and the first thing he remarks is his servile former existence, replete with cowardice and misery. In making a slave of him, that former existence had done to death everything clean, pure and worthwhile that he had started life with, so as to turn him either into a bleating sheep, or an imbecilic master who tramples and destroys anything good to be encountered in himself or in others.

It is at this point only that man awakes to natural freedom, independent of everyone and everything which reduces to ashes anything that defies it, everything that violates nature's purity and captivating beauty, which is made manifest and grows through the autonomous creative endeavor of the individual. It is here only that the individual comes to his senses again and damns his shameful past for once and for all, severing every psychic link with it that hitherto imprisoned his individual and social life with the burden of its servile ascendancy and also, partly, through his own resignation, as encouraged and deceived by the shamans of science.

Henceforth, man makes as much progress from year to year towards a lofty ethical goal — not to be and not to become a shaman himself, some prophet of power over others and no longer to tolerate others wielding power over him — as formerly he was making from generation to generation.

Freed from his heavenly and earthly deities, as well as from all their moral and social prescriptions, man speaks out against and offers actual opposition to man's exploitation of his fellow man and the perversion of his nature, which remains invariably committed to the onward march towards completion and perfection. This rebel, having become conscious of himself and of the circumstances of his oppressed and degraded brethren, thereafter gives expression to his heart and to his reason: he becomes a revolutionary anarchist, the only individual capable of thirsting after freedom, completion and perfection for himself and for the human race, as he tramples underfoot the slavery and social idiocy which has, historically, been embodied by violence — the State. Against that murderer and that organized bandit, the free man in turn organizes along with his fellows, so as to strengthen and espouse a genuinely communist policy in all the common gains made along the road of creation, which is at once grandiose and painful.

The individual members of such groups, by dint of becoming members of them, free themselves from the criminal tutelage of the ruling society, to the extent that they rediscover themselves, that is, they reject all servility towards others, whatever they may have been hitherto: worker, peasant, student or intellectual. In this way they escape from the condition either of a pack-mule, slave, functionary or lackey selling themselves to imbeciles of masters.

As an individual, man gets back to his authentic personality when he rejects false thinking about life and reduces it to ashes, thereby recovering his real rights. It is through this dual operation of rejection and affirmation that the individual becomes a revolutionary anarchist and a conscious communist.

As an ideal of human existence, anarchism is consciously disclosed to each individual as thought's natural aspiration to a free and creative existence, leading on to a social ideal of happiness. In our day, the anarchist society or harmonious human society no longer seems a chimera.

However, like its elaboration and its practical planning, the conception of it seems as yet little in evidence.

As a teaching bearing upon man's new life and its creative development, individually as well as socially, the very idea of anarchism is founded upon the indestructible truth of human nature and on the incontrovertible proofs of the injustice of contemporary society — a veritable permanent blight. Realization of that leads to its advocates — anarchists — finding themselves in conditions of semi- or complete outlawry vis-á-vis the formal institutions of the existing society. Indeed, anarchism cannot be acknowledged as quite lawful in any country: this can be explained in terms of present society's being profoundly impregnated by its servant and master, the State. That band of individuals which has always lived as a parasite upon mankind, by cutting its life up into "slices," has thus identified itself with the State. Whether individually or as a countless mass, man finds himself at the mercy of this band of drones going under the name of "governors and masters," when in reality they are nothing but straightforward exploiters and oppressors.

The great idea of anarchism is not at all to the taste of these sharks who brutalize and enslave the contemporary world, whether they are governments of right or left, bourgeois or statist socialists. The difference between these sharks boils down to the fact that the former are professedly bourgeois — and thus less hypocritical — whereas the latter, the statist socialists of all shades, and among them especially the collectivists who have illegitimately tacked on the label of "communists," namely, the Bolsheviks, hypocritically hide behind the watchwords of "fraternity and equality." The Bolsheviks are ready to give the present society a thousand coats of paint or re-label the systems of domination for some and enslavement for others a thousand times over — in short, to amend the names as their programs may require, without thereby altering the nature of the present society by one iota, even if it means incorporating into their stupid programs compromises between the natural contradictions that exist between domination and servitude. Although they know that these contradictions are insurmountable, they cling to them regardless, for the sole purpose of not letting appear in life the only truly human ideal: libertarian communism.

According to their absurd programs, the statist socialists and communists have decided to "allow" man to emancipate himself socially, without its thereby being feasible for him to manifest that freedom in his social life. As for leaving man to emancipate himself completely, spiritually, in such a way that he may be wholly free to act and to submit only to his own will and the laws of nature alone, although they touch upon that subject, that is out of the question as far as they are concerned. This is the reason why they join their efforts to those of the bourgeois, so that emancipation may never elude their odious supervision. In any event, we know only too well the form that may be taken by "emancipation" awarded by any political authorities.

The bourgeois finds its natural to speak of the toilers as slaves fated to remain such. He will never give encouragement to authentic labor likely to produce something genuinely useful and beautiful, something of benefit to the whole of mankind. Despite the vast capital resources at his disposal in industry and agriculture, he claims not to be able to devise the principles of a novel social existence. The present seems quite adequate to him, for all the powerful kowtow to him: tsars, presidents, governments and virtually all intellectuals and scholars, all who in their turn reduce the slaves of the new society to subjection. "Servants!" the bourgeois cry out to their faithful servitors, "Give to the slaves the pittance which is their due, keep what is due to you for your devoted services, then hold the remainder for us!" In conditions like those, life for them could not be anything other than beautiful! — No, we are not in agreement with you on the above! retort the state socialists and communists. Whereupon they turn to the workers, organizing them into political parties, then inciting them to revolt whilst exhorting them as follows:

Drive out the bourgeois from State power and
give it to us statist socialists and communists,
then we will defend you and set you free.

Bitter, natural enemies of State authority, more than
of the drones and privileged, the toilers give vent to their
hatred, rise in revolt, carry out the revolution, destroy the
power of the State and drive out those wielding it, and
then, either through naiveté or lack of vigilance, they let the
socialists lay hands on it. In Russia, they let the Bolshevik-
Communists lay hands on it like that. These craven Jesuits, these monsters, butchers of freedom, thereupon set
to work to strangle, shoot and crush the people, even
though they were unarmed, just as the bourgeois had done
before them, if not indeed worse. They shot to break the
independent spirit, whether collective or individual, in the
aim of eradicating once and for all from man the spirit of
freedom and the will to create, to leave him a spiritual slave
and physical lackey to a band of villains ensconced in place
of the toppled throne, and not hesitating to deploy killers
to bring the masses to heel and eliminate the recalcitrant.

Man groans underneath the weight of the chains of
socialist power in Russia. He groans in other countries also
beneath the yoke of socialists in cahoots with the bourgeoisie, or even under the yoke of the bourgeoisie alone.
Everywhere, individually or collectively, man groans under the oppressiveness of State power and its political and
economic lunacies. Few people take an interest in his sufferings without simultaneously having second thoughts,
for the executioners, old or new, are spiritually and physically very robust: they can call upon huge effective resources to underpin their hold and crush each and every
person who stands in their way.

Itching to defend his rights to life, liberty and happiness, man seeks to manifest his creative determination by
venturing into the maelstrom of violence. In face of the
uncertain outcome of his fight, he sometimes has a tendency to lower his arms in front of his executioner, at the

very moment when the latter is slipping the noose about his neck, and this when just one bold glance from him would be enough to reduce the executioner to a quivering jelly and call the burdensome yoke once more into question. Unfortunately, man very often prefers to close his eyes at the very moment when the executioner is slipping a noose around his entire life.

Only the man who has successfully rid himself of the chains of oppression and seen all the horrors being perpetrated against the human race can be persuaded that his freedom and that of his neighbor are inviolable, as are their lives, and that his neighbor is his brother. If he is ready to conquer and defend his freedom, to exterminate every oppressor and every executioner (unless the latter renounces his craven trade) then, provided he does not set himself the target in this struggle against the evils of contemporary society of replacing bourgeois power with some other, equally oppressive power — be it socialist, communist or "worker" (Bolshevik) — but rather aims to achieve a really free society, organized on a basis of individual responsibility and guaranteeing all a genuine freedom and equality of social justice for all, that man only is a revolutionary anarchist. He may without fear look upon the works of the executioner-State and, if need be, listen to his verdict, and also pronounce his own by declaring:

> No, it need not be so! Revolt, oppressed brother! Rise up against all State power! Destroy the power of the bourgeoisie and do not replace it with that of the socialists and Bolshevik-communists. Do away with all State power and drive out its champions, for you will never find friends among them.

The power of the statist socialists or communists is every bit as noxious as that of the bourgeoisie. It may even be more so, when it conducts its experiments with the blood and the lives of men. At this point, it does not take long to revert surreptitiously to the premises of bourgeois power: it no longer has any fears about having recourse to the worst of means, lying and deceiving even more than any other power. The ideas of socialism or State communism become redundant: it no longer avails of them, laying hands instead upon any which might help it to cling to power. In the last analysis, it merely uses new means to perpetuate domination and become more cowardly than the bourgeoisie which strings the revolutionary up in public view whilst Bolshevism-communism murders and strangles on the sly.

Any political revolution which has left the bourgeoisie and the state socialists or communists to fight it out is a good illustration of what I have just been saying, especially if one considers the examples of the Russian revolutions of February and October 1917. Having overthrown the Russian empire, the toiling masses consequently felt themselves to be half-liberated politically and sought to complete their liberation. They set about transferring the land confiscated from the great landlords and the clergy to those who worked it or indeed intended to do so without exploitation of another man's labor. In the towns, it was the factories, workshops, printing-works and other social enterprises that were taken in hand by those who worked there. Embroiled in these healthy and enthusiastic endeavors, designed to institute fraternal relations between town and country, the toilers omitted to notice that new governments were being installed in Kiev, Kharkov and Petrograd.

Through its class organizations, the people yearned to lay the foundations of a new, free society intended, as it develops without interference, to eliminate from the body of society all the parasites and all the power exercised by some over others, these being deemed by the toilers to be stupid and harmful.

This approach clearly made headway in the Ukraine, in the Urals and in Siberia. In Tiflis, Kiev, Petrograd and Moscow, in the very heart of the moribund authorities, a similar tendency surfaced. However, always and everywhere, the state socialists and communists had, and still have, supporters aplenty, as well as their hired killers. Among the latter, sad to say, there were also many workers. Abetted by these paid killers, the Bolshevik-Communists put paid to the people's endeavors and in a manner so terrible that even the Medieval Inquisition might feel envious of them!

As for ourselves, knowing the nature of all State power, we told the socialist and Bolshevik leaders:

> Shame on you! You have written and talked so much about the ferocity of the bourgeoisie towards the oppressed. You have been so zealous in your defense of the revolutionary purity and commitment of the toilers struggling for their emancipation and now, having come into power, you turn out to be either the same cowardly lackeys of the bourgeoisie or have become bourgeois yourselves through recourse to its methods, to the extreme that the bourgeoisie stands astounded and pokes fun at you.

Moreover, through the experiences of Bolshevism-Communism, the bourgeoisie has been brought to a realization, in recent years, that the "scientific" chimera of a state socialism proved unable to cope without its methods and indeed, itself. It has grasped the point so well that it pokes fun at its pupils who cannot even live up to its example. It has realized that in the socialist system, the exploitation and organized violence against the bulk of the laboring population do nothing to do away with the debauched life-style and parasitism of the drones, that in fact the exploitation suffers only a name change before growing and being redoubled. And this is what the facts bear out for us. One has only to register the Bolsheviks' rapaciousness and their monopolization of all the revolutionary gains of the people, as well as their police, courts, prisons and armies of jailers, all of them deployed against the revolution. The "red" army continues to be recruited by force! In it one finds the same ranks as before, albeit now given different labels, but even more unaccountable and overbearing.

Liberalism, socialism and State communism are three branches of the same family, resorting to different approaches in order to exercise their power over man, with a view to preventing him from growing fully in the direction of freedom and independence through the devising of a new, wholesome, genuine principle rooted in a social ideal valid for the whole human race.

> Rebel! the revolutionary anarchist exhorts the oppressed. Rise up and eradicate all power over you and within you. And have no truck with the establishment of any new power over others. Be free and defend the freedom of others against all trespass!

In human society, power is particularly exalted by those who have never really lived by their own labor and a wholesome existence, or indeed who no longer live by it or have no wish to live by it. The power of the State will never deliver joy, happiness and fulfillment to any society. Such power was created by drones for the sole purpose of pillage and indulgence of their often murderous violence against those who do produce, through their toil — whether through determination, intelligence or brawn — everything useful and good in man's life.

Whether that power styles itself bourgeois, socialist or Bolshevik-Communist or worker-peasant power, it all comes down to the same thing: it is every whit as damaging to a wholesome and happy individual as it is to society at large. The nature of all State power is everywhere identical: it tends to annihilate the freedom of the individual, turning him, spiritually, into a slave, and physically into a lackey, before putting him to use for the filthiest tasks. There is no such thing as harmless power.

Oppressed brother, banish all power from within you and do not allow any to be established either over you or over your brother, be he near or far!

The really wholesome, joyous life of the individual or group is not built up with the aid of power and programs that seek to enclose it within artificial constructs and written laws. No, it can only be constructed on a basis of individual freedom and its independent creative endeavor, making headway through phases of destruction and construction.

The freedom of every individual is the foundation of the libertarian society: the latter attains wholeness through decentralization and the realization of a common objective: libertarian communism.

Whenever we think of the libertarian communist society, we see it as a grandiose society, harmonious in its human relationships. It is chiefly dependent upon the free individuals banded together into affinity groupings — whether prompted by interest, need or inclination — guaranteeing an equal measure of social justice for all and linking up into federations and confederations.

Libertarian communism is a society that is rooted in the free life of every man, in his untouchable entitlement to infinite development, the elimination of all injustices and all the evils that have hobbled society's progress and perfectibility by splitting it into strata and classes, sources of man's oppression and violence towards his fellow man.

The libertarian society sets itself the target of making everyone's life more beautiful and more radiant, through his labor, his determination and his intellect. In full accord with nature, libertarian communism is, consequently, founded upon man's life made wholly fulfillment, independent, creative and absolutely free. For that reason its adepts appear to live the lives of free and radiant beings.

Labor, universally fraternal relations, love of life, the passion for free creation of beauty, all these values animate

The Struggle Against the State and Other Essays

the life and activity of the libertarian communists. They have no need of prisons, executioners, spies and provocateurs, whom the statist socialists and communists employ in such huge numbers. As a matter of principle, the libertarian communists have no need for the hired brigands and killers of which the prime example and supreme chief is, in the last analysis, the State. Oppressed brother! Prepare yourself for the establishment of that society, through reflection and organized action. Except, just remember that your organization must be solid and consistent in its social activity. The sworn enemy of your emancipation is the State: it is best embodied by the union of these five stereotypes: the property-owner, the soldier, the judge, the priest and the one who serves them all, the intellectual. In most instances, the last-named of these takes it upon himself to demonstrate the "legitimate" entitlement of his four masters to punish the human race, regulate man's life in its every individual and social aspect, and in so doing, distorting the meaning of the natural law in order to codify "historical and juridical" laws, the criminal outpourings of pen-pushers on a retainer.

The enemy is very strong because, for centuries past, he has made his living from rapine and violence: he has the accumulated experience of that, he has overcome internal crises and now he puts on a new face, being threatened with extinction through the emergence of a new science that rouses man from his age-old slumbers. This new science frees man from his prejudices and equips him for self-discovery and discovery of his true place in life, despite all the efforts of the sorcerers' apprentices from that union of the "five" to block his progress down that avenue.

Thus, such a change of face on the part of our enemy, oppressed brother, can be noted, say, in everything that emanates from the chambers of the State's erudite reformers. We have watched a typical example of such a metamorphosis in the revolutions we have witnessed at first-hand. The union of the "five," the State, our enemy, seemed at first to have vanished completely from the face of the earth.

In reality, our enemy merely altered his appearance and found himself new allies who schemed criminally against us: the example of the Bolshevik-Communists in Russia, in the Ukraine, in Georgia and among many Central Asian peoples is very edifying in this regard. This is a lesson that will never be forgotten by the man fighting for his emancipation, for the nightmarish criminality will be engraved in him.

The sole, the surest weapon available to the victim of oppression in his battle against the evil that binds him is the social revolution, a profound leap forward in the direction of human evolution.

Although the social revolution occurs spontaneously, organization smoothes its passage, eases the appearance of breaches in the ramparts erected against it and speeds its coming. The revolutionary anarchist beavers away in the here and now along these lines. Every victim of oppression become sensible of the yoke weighing him down, realizing that this ignominy is crushing the life out of the human race, should come to the aid of the anarchist. Every human being should be aware of his responsibility and see it through by casting out of society all the executioners and parasites from the union of "five," so that mankind may breathe free.

Every man and above all the revolutionary anarchist — as the pioneer inciting struggle for the ideal of freedom, solidarity and equality — ought to bear it in mind that the social revolution, if it is to evolve creatively, requires adequate means, especially ongoing organizational resources, particularly during the phase when, in a spontaneous outburst, it tears slavery up by the roots and plants freedom, affirming every man's entitlement to free and unbounded development. This is the very time when, coming alive to the freedom within and surrounding them, individuals and masses will make bold to act upon the gains of the social revolution, and that revolution will have most need of such organizational resources. For example, revolutionary anarchists played a particularly outstanding role in the Russian revolution, but, not being possessed of the requisite means of action, were unable to see their historical mission through. Moreover, that revolution demonstrated to us the following truth: after having rid themselves of the bonds of slavery, the masses of humanity have no intention of creating new ones. On the contrary: during times of revolution, the masses fetch about for new forms of free associations capable not only of responding to their libertarian instincts, but also of defending their gains should the enemy mount an attack.

Observing this process at work, we were constantly drawn to the conclusion that the most fruitful and most valuable associations could not be other than the commune-unions, the ones whose social resources are conjured up by life itself: the free soviets. Basing himself on that same belief, the revolutionary anarchist hurls himself into selfless action and exhorts the oppressed to join the struggle for free associations. He is convinced that not only must the essential creative organizational precepts be demonstrated: there is also the need to equip oneself with the wherewithal to defend the new life-style against hostile forces. Practice has shown that this has to be pursued most firmly and supported by the masses themselves, in person and on the spot.

In carrying through the revolution, under the impulsion of the anarchism that is innate in them, the masses of humanity search for free associations. Free assemblies always command their sympathy. The revolutionary anarchist must help them to formulate this approach as best they can. For instance, the economic problem of the free association of communes must find full expression in the creation of production and consumer cooperatives, of which the free soviets will be the sponsors. It is through the good offices of the free soviets while the revolution is rippling outwards, that the masses will themselves lay hands upon the entirety of the social heritage: the land, forests, workshops, factories, railways and seaborne transportation, etc., and then, banding together on the basis of interests, affinities or a shared ideal, they will rebuild their social life along the most varied lines to suit their needs and wishes.

It goes without saying that this will be a vicious struggle; it will cost a huge number of lives, for it will pit free humankind against the old world for one last time. There will be no room for hesitation or sentiment. It will be a life or death struggle! At any rate, that is how any man who places any store by his rights and the rights of humankind should think of it, unless he wishes to remain a beast of burden, a slave, as he is compelled to be at the moment.

When healthy reasoning and love of oneself and of others alike gain the ascendancy in life, man will become the authentic author of his own existence.

Organize, oppressed brother, summon all men from plow and workshop, from school and university desk, not forgetting the scholar and the intellectual generally, so that he may venture beyond his chambers and help you along your daunting course. It is true that nine out of ten intellectuals may fail to answer your call or, if they do respond, will do so with the intention of pulling the wool over your eyes, for remember that they are the faithful servants of the union of the "five." Even so, there will be that one in ten who will prove your friend and will help you puncture the deceit of the other nine. As far as physical violence, the brute force of those who govern and legislate, is concerned, you will see it off with violence of your own.

Organize, summon all your brethren to join the movement and insist of all who govern that, of their own volition, they cease their craven profession of regulating the life of man. Should they refuse, rise up, disarm their police, militiamen and the other guard-dogs of the union of the "five." Arrest all governors for as long as need be, tear up and burn their laws! Tear down the prisons, once you have annihilated the executioners and eradicate all State power!

Many paid killers and assassins are in the army, but your friends, the draftees, are there also. Call them to your side and they will come to your aid and help you neutralize the mercenaries.

Once you have all come together into one big family, brethren, we will march together down the path of enlightenment and knowledge, we will leave the shadows behind and stride towards mankind's common ideal: the free and fraternal life, the society wherein no one will be a slave any longer, nor humiliated by anyone.

To the brute violence of our foes we will make reply through the compact force of our insurgent revolutionary army. To incoherence and arbitrariness, we will make reply by erecting our new life upon a foundation of justice, on a basis of individual responsibility, the true guarantor of freedom and social justice for all.

Only the blood-thirsty criminals of the union of the "five" will refuse to join us on the path to innovation: they will try to oppose us so as to cling to their privileges, thereby signing their own death warrant.

Long live this clear, firm belief in the struggle for the ideal of general human harmony: the anarchist society!

Probuzdeniye No. 18, Jan. 1932, pp. 57-63 and no 19-20, Feb.-March 1932, pp. 16-20.

17. Open Letter to Spanish Anarchists

Dear Comrades Carbó and Pestaña,

Convey to our friends and comrades and, through them, to all Spanish workers my encouragement to them not to let their resolution falter in the revolutionary process which has been launched, as well as to make haste in uniting around a practical program drafted along libertarian lines. At all costs there must be no let up in the pace of the masses' revolutionary action. On the contrary, we must rush to help them compel (by force if there is no other way, no other means) the acting republican government which is hindering and distracting the revolution with its absurd decrees to desist from such harmful endeavors.

The Spanish toilers — workers, peasants and working intelligentsia — must unite and display the utmost revolutionary energy so as to conjure into existence a situation whereby the bourgeoisie may be precluded from opposing the seizure of land, factories and full freedoms: a situation that would thus become more and more widespread and irreversible.

It is crucial that no effort be spared to get the Spanish toilers to grasp this and understand that to let this make-or-break moment slip by whilst remaining inactive and making do with the mere passing of splendid resolutions which come to nothing, would be tantamount to unwittingly playing into the hands of the revolution's enemies, allowing them to seize the initiative and giving them time to recover and then to snuff out the revolution that is underway.

To that end, there is a need for a union of libertarian forces, most especially in the shape of the foundation of a great peasant union that would federate with the CNT, and within which anarchists would beaver away indefatigably.

It is also vital that the workers get help to establish, on the spot, organs of economic and social self-direction — free soviets — as well as armed detachments for the defense of the revolutionary social measures that they will inevitably be imposing once they have come to their senses and broken all the chains of their slavish condition. Only in this way and by such broadly social action methods will the revolutionary workers be capable of striking while the iron is hot against the attempt by a new system of exploitation to drive the revolution off course. As I see it, the FAI and the CNT must take this problem seriously and to that end, be able to call upon action groups in every village and town: likewise, they must not be afraid to assume the reins of the strategic, organizational and theoretical revolutionary leadership of the toilers' movement. Obviously they will have to steer clear here of unity with the political parties generally and with the Bolshevik-communists in particular, for I imagine that their Spanish counterparts will be worthy imitators of their Russian mentors. They will follow in the footsteps of the Jesuit Lenin or even of Stalin, not hesitating to assert their monopoly over all the gains of the revolution, with an eye to establishing the power of their party in the country, an aim the effects of which are familiar from the shameful example of Russia: the silencing of all free revolutionary tendencies and of all independent toilers' organizations. Indeed they see themselves as holding power alone and being in a position to control all freedoms and rights in the revolution. So they will inevitably betray their allies and the very cause of the revolution.

The Spanish revolution is the cause of workers the world over and in this undertaking there is no way that there can be any common ground with the party that, in the name of its dictatorship over the country, would have no hesitation in deceiving the workers and laying hands on all their revolutionary gains, in order to emerge as the worst despots and foes of the freedoms and rights of the people.

The Russian precedent must spare you that. May the calamity of Bolshevik communism never take root in the revolutionary soil of Spain!

Long live the union of the workers, peasants and working intellectuals of the whole of Spain!

Long live the Spanish revolution as it strides towards a new world of increasingly liberating gains, under the banner of anarchism!

With my fraternal best wishes,

Nestor Makhno
29 April 1931

Probuzdeniye No. 23-27, June-October 1932, pp. 77-78.

18. On the History of the Spanish Revolution of 1931 — and the Part Played by the Left- and Right-wing Socialists and the Anarchists

Whenever a revolution breaks out — and regardless of its character — (the most important point is that broad masses of workers and peasants should have a hand in it) and its guides, whether a compact group or a scattering of individuals, enjoying a special authority in the eyes of the workers, place themselves above these masses and do not march in step with them and do not earn their trust, waiting for something out of the ordinary to happen or even, worse still, seek to subordinate them by trying to point them along the "only" path to follow, well, the revolution fails to develop thoroughly enough and fails to resolve or even correctly formulate the attendant problems in need of resolution. Then it cannot devise new and additional methods of social action to thwart its enemies and meet the pressing needs: whereupon it is induced to adopt vague directions and gets lost amid their fatal zigzags. At that point, it either perishes under the blows of those against whom it is targeted, or it changes tack, doubles back on its steps and is wound up in accordance with the interests of its internal enemies.

Often, all these considerations have been decisive during the revolutions which have occurred thus far, both in Europe and elsewhere. The same thing has happened in Spain. True, the Spanish revolution of 1931 stands apart from lots of others on account of its very specific features.

It was not unleashed by means of a revolutionary whirl-wind in the towns and countryside, but rather by the bal-lot box. As it proceeded, thanks to the actions of its left-wing elements, it broke free of those initial moorings and entered the vast precincts of the liberating social action of the toilers. Whilst it nonetheless finished to the advantage of authoritarian elements, and proved tragic for the fate of the workers and many revolutionaries, as well as for what these had managed to achieve, the responsibility for that lies largely with the Spanish left-wing political groupings. That unfortunate denouement can be chalked up to the authoritarian and the anti-authoritarian socialists, which is to say to our libertarian communist and anarcho-syndi-calist comrades.

The responsibility of the right-wing state socialists consists of their having been tied from the outset to the bourgeois party of Alcala Zamora. True, the grassroots mili-tants of the party, especially the workers, did not want to hear talk of this policy, especially as they were not aware of the hidden negotiations of their party's "bigwigs" with the bourgeoisie, negotiations directed at their assuming joint power, albeit at the price of sacrificing the revolution. It was only when the socialist workers found themselves under questioning from other workers about their party's policy, and had no idea how to reply, that their leaders hypo-critically strutted like peacocks before the bourgeoisie, strik-ing a little fear into its representatives by declaring them-selves ready to seize power alone with the aid of the work-ers only. This double dealing by the socialist leaders re-garding the revolution, mounted despite the pretenses by taking cognizance of the aspirations of the workers as rep-resented by other social revolutionary organizations, none-theless sowed the most utter confusion in the minds and understanding of the workers as far as the developing revo-lution was concerned, and in the last analysis it eroded the best and most combative features of their struggle, every-thing that had enabled them to score a complete and en-thusiastic victory over the monarchists and the king.

The Spanish toilers sensed instinctively that the time had come for new and free forms of social living. The right-wing socialist "bigwigs" pretended outwardly to congratulate themselves on this, but in fact and in secret they worked to disappoint these aspirations, and in so doing they did enormous harm to the first steps of the revolution.

The guilt of the Bolshevik-communists — they who are "further to the left than the left" of the state socialists, so to speak — resides in their having done nothing on behalf of the cause of real emancipation of the workers, but instead only for their own sordid and petty partisan interests. They saw the revolution as a means whereby they might, at their ease, stuff proletarian heads with the most demagogic promises and then, having sucked them into the authoritarian vortex, use them bodily to hoist their filthy party dictatorship into position over the country. When they realized that their demagogic ploys were making no headway with the toilers, they suborned or deceived a few adventurist elements into organizing violent demonstrations, whilst drawing the unarmed workers into them. These demonstrations, however, brought them no success either. Blood flowed freely during these workers' defeats, dreamt up by people who kept well out of the action. All of which merely strengthened the coalition between the right wing socialists and Alcala Zamora and the bourgeoisie, bolstering it not just against the left's "would-be dictators," but also against the revolution generally.

As for the Bolshevik "communists," they belong to the same Marxist-Leninist school as their Russian counterparts: they are nothing more than Jesuits and traitors to all who struggle against Capital and for the emancipation of the proletariat whilst refusing to pass between their Caudine Forks. During the Spanish revolution of 1931, they were not strong enough — and still are not — to display their treachery openly. Even so, they have successfully mounted several provocations and peddled calumnies, not so much against the bourgeoisie as against their political adversaries on the left. That fact partly accounts for the difficulty the revolution has experienced in ridding itself of bourgeois thinking and bourgeois leaders, for it has had to fight simultaneously against the demoralization peddled by these "leftist" traitors. The latter operate on the behalf of their dictatorship and not for the sake of real social freedom, which blends the solidarity and equality of opinion of all who have made the radical break with the onerous past of exploitation and who are striding right now towards a new world.

Spanish libertarian communists and anarcho-syndicalists have a particular responsibility in the shaping of events, above all because they departed from their basic principles in taking an active part in that revolution, so as to wrest the initiative from the liberal bourgeoisie, no doubt, but whilst remaining, regardless, on the latter's parasitical class terrain. They have, for one thing, taken absolutely no notice of the requirements of our age, and for another, they have under-estimated the scale of the resources available to the bourgeoisie in containing and eliminating all who create trouble for it.

What has stopped anarchists from putting their beliefs into practice, so as to turn a bourgeois republican revolution into a social revolution?

In the first place, the absence of a specific and detailed program has prevented them from achieving unity of action, the unity that determines the expansion of the movement during a period of revolution and of its influence over everything around it.

Secondly, our Spanish comrades, like many comrades elsewhere, regard anarchism as an itinerant church of freedom. . . . That attitude regularly prevents them from arriving at the desired times and places at the working structures essential to the economic and social organization whose duty it is to weave multiple connections between the everyday and global struggle of the toilers. This has thwarted them, on this occasion, from accomplishing the historical task that devolves upon anarchism in time of revolution. For all the prestige they enjoyed in the eyes of the workers in the country, Spanish libertarian communists and anarcho-syndicalists have failed to tilt in the direction of revolution the minds of masses dithering between their sympathy with revolution and a petit-bourgeois outlook. They ought to have been converted into activists for the spread and defense of the revolution. Instead of which, feeling themselves surrounded by relative freedom, the anarchists, like so many petit-bourgeois, have indulged themselves in interminable discussions. By word of mouth and in writing, they have expounded absolutely freely on all manner of topics: they have held rallies galore, with fine professions of faith, but they have overlooked the fact that those who supplanted the king spent that time entrenching their power to the best of their ability.

Unfortunately, in this regard, not a thing was done at the appropriate time, even though that was as vital as could be, given that the occasion was ideal and the circumstances favorable. At that point, the Spanish anarchists had real opportunities — a lot more than all the other revolutionary groupings in the country — to settle in practice upon a strategy that would have brought the revolution a step closer. The CNT expanded its membership at a dizzying rate and became, for all who labor, the spokesman and the forum through which the toilers' age-old hopes might at last find expression.

In order to play up this active role of our movement even more, the bourgeoisie and its power should have been felled and its influence upon the revolutionary movement eradicated utterly. Does this mean that our Spanish comrades achieved nothing along these lines during that revolutionary year of 1931? Certainly not. They did all in their power to convert the political revolution into social revolution. Heroically, they shouldered the sacrifices of that, and even now that the revolution has been smothered, many of them are still enduring the rigors of repression. However, all such sacrifices have been in vain, to the extent that they were not made for the sake of suitable objectives. And all, let me repeat, because anarchism possesses no hard and fast program, because the anarchist activities that have been carried out have been, and are still, conducted amidst the most utter dispersion, rather than springing from a tactical unity determined and enlightened by a theoretical unity, by a single shared goal. It is for these specific reasons that the Spanish anarchists have not been able to bring their endeavors to fruition and it is this that induced the ones whose convictions were weakest to issue the celebrated "Manifesto of the Thirty" — quite ill-timed — in the name of its authors' "heightened sense of responsibility." The most determined and intrepid militants, the ones that do not merely peddle their ideas but also go to the lengths of dying for them, those ones languish in filthy dungeons, in the holds of vessels deporting them to distant shores, to hostile lands.

Such, in broad outline, are the omissions, errors and shortcomings fatal for revolutionary activity that have been perpetrated by Spanish leftist groupings, at a decisive moment that comes but rarely in history and which has brought the Spanish revolution to its present straits. All those groups therefore carry the responsibility for the situation.

What conclusions the statist socialists, they who can do nothing better than play the lackeys of the bourgeoisie, whilst seeking to make lackeys of their own of other revolutionaries, will draw from this I cannot tell. As far as revolutionary anarchists are concerned, I believe they have food for thought here, if they are to be spared in the future [whether in Spain or elsewhere] from a repetition of these same mistakes: finding themselves in the revolution's advanced outposts without access to the resources necessary for defense of the masses' revolutionary gains against the bitter onslaughts of their bourgeois and authoritarian socialist foes.

Obviously, revolutionary anarchists must not have recourse to the methods of Bolsheviks as some have occasionally been tempted to do, even to the extent of urging the establishment of "close contact" with the Bolshevik state (as the "innovator" Arshinov has lately argued). Revolutionary anarchists have nothing to look for in Bolshevism: they have a revolutionary theory of their own that is indeed very rich, and which lays down tasks utterly at odds with those of the Bolsheviks in the life and struggle of the toiling classes. They cannot reconcile their goals with the goals of Pan-Bolshevism, which thrusts itself so savagely, by ruble and bayonet, into the lives of the toilers in the USSR, deliberately ignoring their rights and turning them into compliant slaves, incapable of independent reflection, or thinking for themselves about their welfare and the welfare of the other toilers in the world.

No matter how devoted it may be to the movement's cause, no anarchist individual or group can carry out the tasks described all unaided. All attempts made thus far testify to that. Why is understandable: no individual or group can, unaided, unite our movement, nationally or internationally. These mammoth and crucial tasks can only be accomplished by an international libertarian think-tank. That is what I told Rudolf Rocker and Alexander Berkman in Berlin nearly seven years ago now. And I reaffirm it all the more staunchly now, now that many libertarians openly acknowledge — after a whole series of fruitless attempts to devise something practical — that there is no other way of arriving at a program shaped by and attuned to our times and our resources, than by the calling of a preparatory conference, (involving those militants most active and committed in matters theoretical and practical alike) the task of which would be formulate the theses that would respond to the anarchist movement's vital issues, theses thrashed out in anticipation of an international anarchist congress. The latter in turn would develop and complement these theses. In the wake of that congress, these theses would amount to a definite program and solid reference point for our movement, a reference point with a validity in every country. Which would rescue our movement from reformist and muddle-headed deviations and invest it with the necessary potency to become the vanguard of contemporary revolutions.

True, this is no easy undertaking: however, determination and solidarity from those who can and who wish to carry it off will greatly facilitate this endeavor. Let this undertaking commence, for our movement cannot but gain by it!

Long live the fraternal and shared hopes of all Anarchist militants that they may see the realization of that grand undertaking — the endeavor of our movement and of the social revolution for which we struggle!

France 1931

Probuzdeniye No. 30-31, January-February 1933, pp. 19-23

BIBLIOGRAPHICAL AFTERWORD

ALEXANDRE SKIRDA

Among the articles by Nestor Makhno left out of this anthology, we might mention the one on the peasantry and the Bolsheviks,[1] where he sets out the (in fact, quite well-known) socio-economic differentials between the wealthy peasants, or *kulaks*, the middle peasantry or *serednyakis*, the poor peasants or *bednyakis*, and the farm laborers or *batrakis*. Categories that the Bolsheviko-Stalinist policy of developing rural capitalism in the 1920s tended to reduce to its extremities alone: to the kulaks and the batrakis, to the detriment of the overwhelming majority of the peasantry. We know, here, that from 1929 to 1934, this policy was escalated in such a way as to lead to the utter dispossession of the peasants of their land, and this at the price of the holocaust of its times, which has been underplayed thus far, for this "de-kulakisation" cost the lives of 15 million victims, according to reliable estimates. Let it be noted that this was the real epilogue to the civil war, for this genocide affected primarily those regions of Russia, the Ukraine and Don and the Volga, which had been the areas then most refractory to the new regime. As for the results of this demented warfare against people on the land, these were extremely retrograde: the kulaks, previously a tiny minority, were replaced by the Kulak-State, whilst the survivors of the slaughter, re-christened "kolkhozians" — which is to say, farm workers — were reduced in their circumstances to the status of real State serfs. Unfortunately, Makhno did not have access to adequate information about this criminal policy on the part of Stalin and his henchmen, which is what makes his piece obsolete.

In his *Open Letter to the Central Committee of the Russian CP*[2] which appeared in 1928, Makhno expressed his outrage at a misrepresentation of his dealings with Bela Kun, at the time of his second treaty with the Red Army in September 1920. He clarified another historical point in his *How the Bolsheviks Lie*.[3] He re-established the truth about the anarchist sailor Anatoly Zhelezniakov, who broke up the sitting of the Constituent Assembly in January 1918. Makhno defended that action and explained that Zhelezniakov, a Black Sea sailor and delegate to Kronstadt, had played one of the most active roles in 1917. Makhno merely expressed regret that the fiery sailor, who enjoyed great prestige among his colleagues, had not simultaneously seen fit to dismiss Lenin and his "Soviet of People's Commissars" which "would have been historically vital and would have helped unmask the stranglers of the revolution in good time." In a short piece, *England's Policy and the World Tasks of the Revolutionary Toilers*[4], he lashed British imperialism and floated the idea that there was no way of resisting its plans for the revolution and the USSR, by virtue of the fact that, inside the USSR, "there is neither freedom of speech, nor of assembly, nor of the press, nor of independent organization for workers." As a result, there was not a thing worth defending as long as there was this denial of justice vis à vis their "rights to be free and responsible."

We might also cite his *Appeal on Behalf of the Anarchist Black Cross*, where he labored the need for aid for libertarians around the world, and in particular in the USSR, persecuted for their beliefs.

For access in French to all Makhno's output, one has only to look to his Memoirs — nigh on six hundred pages of them — which is to say, seek out some publisher to publish them, something we have not been successful in doing, despite numerous fruitless overtures thus far. It might also be desirable if Arshinov's *History of the Makhnovist Movement* was republished in a new translation as soon as possible (the translation by Voline being, occasionally, flawed), again necessitating the goodwill of some heavy-weight publisher. Those two books would certainly not be going over old ground, either with regard to each other, or to my monograph on Makhno, for the latter was actually planned as a complementary project.

This strikes us as the appropriate point to review some publications and new information which have come to out attention since our book (the product of eighteen years of research and authentication, which is to say, no spur of the moment affair, which is more than can be said for most publications in the field) was published. Broadly speaking, we have a parade of the sensational aspects of certain charges or claims, in such a way as to push into the background the true significance of the Makhnovist insurgent movement. This is the case, say, with the publication by Pavel Litvinov (grandson of Stalin's Foreign Affairs minister) of a samizdat text (a self-published, clandestine text) entitled *Nestor Makhno and the Jewish Question*.[5] The author strives to show that Makhno was never an anti-Semite: quite the opposite, in fact, he "deserves to have his memory respected and honored by the Jews." That would be an attractive approach, were it not that he is trying doors that are already gaping wide open, for, as we have indicated, even Bolshevik historical writings have always rebutted that absurd allegation. Furthermore, Litvinov connects this issue with the re-emergence of Jewish nationality and indeed with the attempt to establish a revolutionary Jewish "Zion" in the Ukraine! What is rather positive though is that Litvinov seizes upon the opportunity to rehearse the chief characteristics and achievements of the Makhnovist movement, especially its active role in the defeat of the Whites. We might note that the essential sources he uses have been published outside Russia: some are drawn from

Russian anarchist reviews and works published in France and the United States during the 1920s and 1930s: which is to say that these have, in spite of everything, achieved their purpose by helping to re-establish the true facts of the matter. Aside from the odd inaccuracy — Makhno working in Paris as a cinema technician! — Litvinov's work should be read, especially in Israel and by Jewish readers, given that many of them are still believers in "tales" about Makhno. On the other hand, it has nothing new to offer Western readers with access to much more exhaustive texts and writings on the topic: so it is hard to understand the sensational publicity that certain French and Italian anarchists have afforded him.[6] Maybe this is because, for a very long time, there was a dearth of historical and theoretical studies of anarchism, which explains why many anarchists have become "a ready market" and applaud the moment that some academic or anybody outside of the movement and not sharing its ideas deigns to show some interest in Anarchy!

We have also come by a copy of another handwritten text in Russian, dealing with the life of Leon Zadov-Zinkovsky, commander of the unit that smuggled a seriously wounded Makhno into Rumania in August 1921. The manuscript's author, one Jacob Gridin, presents himself as a former member of the NKVD (the Cheka was at first renamed the GPU, then NKVD, before adopting the current straightforward title of KGB) who has emigrated to Israel. According to Gridin, Zadov — who had been in charge of the Makhnovist intelligence service for a while — allegedly contacted the GPU during his exile in Rumania and rendered them stalwart services. In particular he is supposed to have lured a captain from French Counter-espionage into an ambush in the Ukraine and murdered him in his sleep, all to demonstrate his bona fides to the GPU and secure his own rehabilitation, as well as that of his brother. This little spy story even includes a pretty young exploited widow whom Zadov supposedly set himself the task of consoling! The edge to the whole thing is that it is alleged here that Zadov is alleged to have been issued with orders from his superiors in Moscow to "liquidate" Makhno, who is supposed to have been staying in 1922 in one of the best hotels in Warsaw (in reality, he was enjoying the "delights" of a long and uncomfortable stay in the political prison in the city!). Zadov is supposed to have accomplished his mission successfully and to have lived in comfort until the "nasty" Stalinist purges of 1938, when he fell into the trap.

As we have no knowledge about the real fate of Zadov, there is every scope for embroidery upon his fate: however, there is rather too much unlikeliness here and we should remember, first, that in Bolshevik studies Zadov and his brother are portrayed as the executors of Makhno's "dirty work," and above all as implacable killers of Bolsheviks: second, that they had been convinced anarchist militants since 1905, something that had earned them several years in tsarist prisons, and third, that they had repeatedly proved their commitment to the Makhnovist movement's cause.

All of this makes us very skeptical about such absurdities about them, unless there is some confusion with quite different individuals. Moreover, further revelations along similar lines are to be expected of Soviet Jewish émigrés, for a fair number of them are either, as is the case with Gridin, ex-members of the GPU, or privileged members of the State apparatus and other sectors of the regime, or indeed the children or parents of such. Obviously there can be no question of placing the slightest credence in misinformation exercises of this sort, unless we can be very sure that there is the documentary evidence or tangible proof to back up their ramblings.[7]

In our book, we made reference to the existence of a handwritten set of memoirs on Makhno by Ida Mett, a member of the *Dyelo Truda* group from 1925 to 1928. One small press has had the splendid idea of turning these out as a 28-page pamphlet (out of the original six and a quarter pages!), with the addition of a few personal remarks on the "radicality of Nestor Makhno, wherein he shows himself to be resolutely modern, thereby outstripping practically and historically the anarchist ideology. For Makhno, the revolution cannot in any way be the authentication of any ideology — even be it anarchist — but spells the doom of all ideologies."[8] For some years now, it has been fashionable to bandy the word 'ideology' about indiscriminately in every direction, but if one takes the word to mean a coherent view of life and society, it would be a good idea to compare these glib, empty assertions with the views spelled out plentifully in the writings of Makhno as set out in the foregoing anthology. As for Ida Mett's text, we have already outlined its limitations. Some of its remarks are cringe-making: Makhno was "jealous of the Jews," but "had it in him to be a Jew's friend without any effort of will"(?) and was also "jealous of intellectuals" and, more to the point, "jealous" of the careers of the Red generals Budyenny and Voroshilov, so much so that "his head was willy nilly, filled notions that he too could have made a Red Army general. Yet he himself never said as much to me."(!) Such a "telepathic" analysis does much to undermine the impact of such an evaluation and may even come within a hair's breadth of common calumny and tittle-tattle: it would be better left unsaid. Ida Mett, whom we ourselves knew, deserves to be remembered by other, more pertinent writings.

We come now to one of the most intriguing bibliographical novelties. In our biography of Makhno, we mentioned the existence of hitherto unpublished manuscripts by Voline to which we had been unable to gain access. These had been in the possession of Rosa Dubinsky, widow of the first publisher of Voline's posthumous *The Unknown Revolution* and then seized *manu military* by Voline's eldest son, Igor Eichenbaum, who at the time held political views far removed from his father's. On the basis of what Rosa

Dubinsky has told us, the historian Daniel Guerin seems to have played a questionable role at that time. He has since sent us a denial wherein he claims that "this matter proceeded unbeknownst to him."[9] Hereby noted.

We also learned later that there were several copies of these manuscripts in circulation: one with Daniel Guerin, then the secretariat for History of the French Anarchist Federation, and, finally, a copy was placed by Leo Eichenbaum, Voline's second son, with the 'Sound and Picture Archive' set up by Roland Fornari.[10] Thanks to the kindness of the latter, we were able to consult these famous unpublished notes by Voline. What do they contain? Well, to our great amazement, there is, for a start, and above all, the conclusion to *The Unknown Revolution*, which all four of the successive editions of the book deliberately discarded! The text is quite substantial — a hundred and ten pages — and only that part dealing with the Voline-Trotsky meeting in New York, a little before they returned to Russia in 1917, was used by Daniel Guerin in the latest edition of his anthology *Ni Dieu, ni Maître*. Given that he also saw to the publication of the most recent editions of *The Unknown Revolution*, we asked him why these had been deprived of the "conclusion" which was a natural part of the book. His answer to us was that the decision had been made jointly with Igor Eichenbaum, because it struck them that the conclusion's contents "weakened" the remainder of the book. Having read it in our turn, we are not of that mind, for it seems to us to fit perfectly with the psycho-moral analyses of Voline and, whereas he is mistaken in depicting world events "from 1914 up to September 1947" as the "destructive period of the world revolution," the constructive phase being due to "pass a lot quicker," mistakes are still possible, but there cannot, as we see it, be any case for censoring a posthumous work of its "conclusion," which ought to make sense of the whole thing. It is our hope that in some forthcoming edition of the book, this lacuna may be well and truly filled.

Those unpublished papers also include Voline's correspondence from the period towards the end of his life, where he touches upon the matter that concerns us here. In a letter to one Henri, dated 4.11.1944 in Marseilles, he rounded upon someone called Frémont who was alleged to have "peddled rumors about his relations with Makhno." Frémont had had it from "Makhno's own lips that, from a certain point onwards, he and I had not been on as friendly terms as previously. It may even be the case that Makhno turned him against me somewhat," and Frémont had supposedly made the "silly charge" against him that he had "stolen some documents from Makhno." As "formal and palpable proof of the nonsensicality of that crude concoction" Voline cited three arguments in his defense.

1. He claimed to have "sacrificed two full years of his activities, in 1921-1923, to bringing out Arshinov's *History of the Makhnovist Movement*," and he added, "And I do mean 'sacrificed,' for I could have devoted my free time to my own literary output as I was pressed to do and as I was interested in doing."

2. He had taken a back seat in deference to Arshinov for he himself had spent only six months with the Makhnovist movement, whereas Arshinov had been with it right to the end and was thus better "qualified to write a history of it." Later he simply made use of that history and made do with adding a few personal anecdotes in that part of his *The Unknown Revolution* dealing with the Makhnovist movement. That amounts only to a banal statement of the facts as far as any alert reader is concerned, but it is good to find Voline himself making the point.

3. He refers to his work as 'literary editor' of Volumes II and III of Makhno's memoirs which appeared in Russian in 1936 and 1937. Followed by the transla-

tions into French of his forewords to both volumes, as well as part of his introduction to the Makhnovist movement, lifted from *The Unknown Revolution*.

Voline closed a second letter to Henri on 11.11.1944 with the wish that his clarifications "will satisfy comrades' curiosity" and "prove (to them) that the lies about my conduct are simply the result of a crude and stupid calumny capitalizing upon the ignorance of many comrades regarding the truth of the matter." Without knowing more about the precise content of this "calumny" we can only note Voline's arguments and leave the individual reader to make of them what he will.

Let us make special note of Voline's explanation of the fate of Makhno's manuscripts: Galina Kuzmenko, Makhno's wife, was forced to burn her husband's trunk during the German occupation and brought the fact to Voline's attention before leaving for Germany in 1942. We might note her thoughtlessness in doing so; she would have been better advised to entrust them to trustworthy friends or to some library.

In other letters to Marie Louise (Berneri?) Voline outlines the complete story of his writings on the Russian revolution, in fact of the gestation of *The Unknown Revolution*. He also promises there a forthcoming work on Makhno, but admits finding problems "getting to grips with it." He was depending upon making use of the notes that he had used for lectures on Makhno in 1935-36. His TB denied him the time to do so and he succumbed to it shortly afterwards, leaving the project at the notes and drafts stage, all of it nonetheless amounting to some 236 pages, partly typed. Let us have a look at the contents.

The text is entitled "Makhno, a Contribution to Studies of the Enigma of the Personality." Drafted in 1945, it deals in broad terms with the Russian revolution and furnishes autobiographical details about Voline himself. Its primary interest for our purposes is its disclosure of

Voline's input into Arshinov's *History of the Makhnovist Movement*. It was on Voline's insistence that Arshinov mentioned the movement's flaws and those of Makhno himself, after he had told him that "set alongside the tremendous positive aspects to the movement, what few shortcomings there may have been are really of no consequence" (pages 31, 45 and 126). According to Voline this 'overlooking' of the movement's weaknesses is very much to be regretted because these "in his estimation, outweigh the positive sides of it." That critique sets the tone for his whole approach: he switches back and forth between eulogy and the most acerbic criticism, for instance, in a thumbnail sketch of Makhno: "He was an extremely complex personality, 'muddled' might be the right word: a sort of formidable 'raw' genius, replete with flaws, boorishness and sophistication on a par with his marks of genius. . . ." "Beyond question, he is to be numbered in the Russian revolution among that type of personality that one never manages to understand completely, personalities that remain in History forever a little 'elusive'. . . Enormous positive aspects coexisting alongside profound negative traits. . . ." (page 38).

In an unfinished chapter entitled "the nub of the matter," Voline upbraids the existence among the "Ukrainian peasantry, as indeed among peasants (and in fact manual workers generally) all over the world, of a hybrid feeling of diffidence, contempt and sullen hostility that can sometimes boil over into acute fits of hatred, vis à-vis intellectuals, 'non-manual' workers and 'non-peasants.' He then denounces the "very widespread and harmful prejudice among revolutionary militants:" "concealing from the 'public' and from ordinary party militants for as long as they can manage it, the weak sides, 'shadows,' shortcomings and deficiencies of the movement." For his part, he had, with "desperate studiousness and in dribs and drabs" catalogued the "dark sides" of Makhno's personality: in 1938, he "was already in possession of a fair bit of information," but, "by the time he had reached the end of his work (late 1941), knew a lot more. . . ." We might wonder at these belated revelations for, as he himself admits, although he had spent six months on Makhno's company in 1919-1920, he had not "known a thing about the personal, intimate life that would have afforded him an insight into the very depths of the personality (of Makhno)." Furthermore, Makhno "had never made the slightest gesture to strike up a more personal friendship with him." Thus, in order to unlock his true personality, he would use as his chief source the confidences of Galina Kuzmenko, Makhno's wife, who was contradicted, it seems, by certain "Makhnovist commanders" who had fled to France (unfortunately, Makhno never named these) while allegedly looking upon her as a "mismatch" with Makhno.

Voline outlines a very eulogistic sketch of Makhno's good qualities: "I should say a speedy and thorough grip of the truth, which he managed to divine from life overall. . . . "A precise, acute and never-weakening attention to everything that he regarded as significant in life, whether his own or life in general . . . possession of an extremely solid and luminous over-arching idea, is also a mark of genius." "A boundless audacity and temerity with regard not just to fighting but to life as a whole. . . . He strove to make life what he wanted it to be." "A specific talent for fighting, by which I do not mean a military talent . . . he never lost his sang-froid, his daring and he conducted himself with such simplicity and precision and simultaneously with clear, cool tactics until such time as his object was achieved." However, as a "lop-sided man of genius, whose nervousness also was in excess of the norm," the more Makhno "learned of the marks of genius, the more he knew of its high points and of its lows" (pages 58-63).

After these roses, the thorns. Voline notes that Makhno and he were temperamentally incompatible, so much so that, when Makhno had him released from the Cheka prison in October 1920, he hesitated before joining him in the Ukraine. Furthermore, according to him, Makhno had an annoying habit of flourishing his revolver at the slightest pretext, even to the extent of threatening his future comrade with it, perhaps to "test his mettle"(?) as well as members of the Makhnovist movement's soviet, and above all, of gunning down where they stood certain deserters from the front or insurgents guilty of outrages. He supposedly killed people "without having delved into their case and without knowing if they were innocent or guilty" (pages 138). If there is any substance to this, that reproach strikes us as the most significant of Voline's criticisms for, as far as the rest goes, we seem to be dealing with something of an obsession on his part, deriving probably from the run-ins they had had as émigrés, both personally (Makhno had accused Voline of dishonesty) and theoretically (Voline supported the Anarchist Synthesis whilst Makhno was an enthusiast of the Platform).

We might also note a few surprising inaccuracies in Voline's information; he has Makhno dying a year earlier than in fact he did and credits him with having had as his real name the pseudonym — Mikhnienko — under which he had declared himself on his arrival in France. These mix-ups and recriminations might perhaps be explicable in terms of Voline's circumstances at the time when he was drafting most of these notes: under the German occupation, in Marseilles, he had every reason to fear the Gestapo and the Petainist *Milice* and well knew the rigors and deprivation of clandestine life. However it seems to us that the key to the animosity between the pair can be traced to the contrast to which we referred earlier between the activist peasant and the moralizing intellectual unconnected with social practice. [11] Voline appears also to have nurtured resentment because he recalled that in Berlin in 1925, seeing Makhno again for the first time in several years, he told him that "Arshinov, an intellectual and Makhno a peasant" were a "team" and that they had to remain "inseparable." Makhno supposedly would not listen to him[12] and "threw it all up" by "getting maybe more drunk than before." His was "undoubtedly a nature with the talents of a genius, capable of actively and doggedly pursuing whatever goal he had set himself, a man who had a marvelous know-how and who could at the same time topple from such heights into the deepest depths, until he turned into a 'human derelict'(!)" (Page 75.) Likewise, in the Ukraine he had refused to suffer his "moral influence"(page 142) preferring that of the "camarilla" made up of a section of the Makhnovist commanders. For all his "qualities," Makhno remained, as far as Voline was concerned, "an ignorant, uncultivated, uneducated fellow" (page 60), especially as he had an "aversion to anything that was not peasant. Being himself 100 percent peasant, he was completely familiar with peasant life and inclined to criticize anyone who was not a peasant. He did not have much confidence in workers because the worker, according to him, had already been so to speak demoralized by the mad, bad life in the towns and in industry where he stood alongside the bosses. He had even less confidence in intellectuals and poked fun at them. Given that, it was very hard to talk to him about the flaws of his organization because he retorted with all sorts of mockery that left you nonplused and denied you every chance of settling matters one way or another." (Page 134.) Elsewhere, Voline mentions these traits of Makhno's character even more explicitly: "blind *confidence* in the peasantry, *distrust* of all the other classes of society: a certain *contempt* for intellectuals, even anarchist ones." (Page 49.)

This is the nub of the matter and the spot where the knife went into Voline! As a "morally irreproachable" intellectual, he had high hopes of acting as a keeper of conscience, in order to steer it along the "right road." Instead of which Makhno had refused his advice, perhaps mockingly, in order to fall back upon his base instincts as a "muzhik"! As if to confirm this, whilst in exile in Paris, Voline one day labeled him a muzhik (which must have been an insult equivalent in his eyes to "ignorant brute" or some such) and an anarchist honor board had to be assembled to smooth over the falling out. [13]

In fact, out of the 236 hand-written pages supposedly dealing with Makhno, only a very few relate directly to the subject, most being given over to all manner of digressions. To back up his criticisms, Voline cites some specific instances in which he was an eye-witness or a protagonist: the remainder is only impressions, hearsay evidence and inconsequential confidences from Makhno's wife, which seems little very slight basis for the gravity of the charges he brings. It strikes us as obvious then that the credence to be placed in these should be measured alongside the degree of enmity that he bore Makhno. He would have been better advised to describe in detail, not just a few episodes, but the entirety of his time with the Makhnovist insurgents, unless he spent that time "cloistered" in his cultural activities and deliberately avoided mingling with the "muzhiks" and speaking directly and pertinently to them, without having to rely upon second-hand information. He could also have reviewed the circumstances that prefaced his arrival in the insurgent camp: it was Makhno in person who despatched a detachment to rescue him from the clutches of the Petliurist partisans. It was also at the suggestion and instigation of Makhno that he was appointed chairman of the Revolutionary Military Soviet of the insurgent movement for several months, and again Makhno who made his release one of the conditions upon the implementation of the military and political treaty agreed with the Bolsheviks in 1920. He also omits to mention the "deposition" he made before a Chekist investigating magistrate, a "deposition" critical, to say the least, of the Makhnovists, for soviet historians have since used it to discredit them.[14]

In substance, all of these random jottings, awash with sweeping generalizations, strike us as revealing more about the author's personality than about Makhno's: which is probably why they have remained unpublished thus far. However, despite their obvious exaggerations, these texts deserve to be better known, as certain passages from them are of definite value for the period. As for Makhno's "true" personality, that emerges sufficiently from all his writings — memoirs and articles alike — for us to avoid reference to the anarchist "rumor mill" in search of further "sensational" disclosures.

In the context of this bibliographical update, let us note the oral testimony of the historian Oleg Koshchuk, who is of Ukrainian extraction. His mother was interned in Poland in the same camp as Makhno and remembers that certain Petliurists wanted to attempt the libertarian's life, probably remembering some skirmish that went against them. At which point, it was intimated to them by highly placed nationalist leaders that any move against Makhno would be construed as an act of hostility towards the Ukrainian cause. Despite their political differences, ethnic solidarity came into play here to unite Ukrainians from both banks of the river Dniepr.

NOTES

1. *Dyelo Truda* February-March 1928, No. 33-34, pp. 7-9.

2. *Dyelo Truda* June-July 1928, No. 37-38, pp. 10-12.

3. *Dyelo Truda* March 1927, No. 22, p.12.

4. *Dyelo Truda* July-August 1927, No. 10-12.

5. P. Litvinov *Nestor Makhno et la question juive* 21 typewritten pages dated 18 June 1982, Moscow. This text has been published by the magazine *Vremya i my* (*Time and Us*) in Israel, No. 17, 1983.

6. *A Revista Anarchica*, 8 November 1983, Milan (Italy).

7. A 16-page manuscript.

8. Ida Mett, *Souvenirs sur Nestor Makhno*, Paris 1983, pp. 25-26.

9. Letter to the author, 27 December 1982.

10. Address: 5 rue Caplat, 75018 Paris.

11. *Nestor Makhno, le cosaqu de l'Anarchie* pp. 323-326 and 358-360

12. Perhaps he did not agree with the definition of this anarchist "holy trinity?"

13. Minutes of the meeting can be found in the papers of Rene Fuchs. See Archives Jean Maitron.

14. Not that this stopped them from upbraiding him as well: the most recent one, Semanov, even alleges, apropos his "ed-

iting" of Makhno's Memoirs, that he "was a parasite" on Makhno. S.N. Semanov "The Makhnovshchina and its collapse" in *Voprosy Istorii* (Questions of History) Moscow, 1966, No. 9, p. 52 (note 81). Let us point out also a little known something: Voline's brother, Boris Eichenbaum (1886-1959) was the theoretician of the "formalist" school, and later an important literary critic under the Stalin regime.

Friends
of AK Press

In the last 12 months, AK Press has published around 15 new titles. In the next 12 months we should be able to publish roughly the same, including new work by Murray Bookchin, CRASS, Daniel Guerin, Noam Chomsky, Jello Biafra, Stewart Home, a new anthology of situationist writings, new audio work from Noam Chomsky, plus more. However, not only are we financially constrained as to what (and how much) we can publish, we already have a huge backlog of excellent material we would like to publish sooner, rather than later. If we had the money, we could easily publish 30 titles in the coming 12 months.

Projects currently being worked on include previously unpublished early anarchist writings by Victor Serge; more work from Noam Chomsky, Murray Bookchin and Stewart Home; Raoul Vaneigem on the surrealists; a new anthology of computer hacking and hacker culture; a short history of British Fascism; the collected writings of Guy Aldred; a new anthology of cutting edge radical fiction and poetry; an updated version of the seminal anthology of contemporary anarchist writings, *Re-Inventing Anarchy*; new work from Freddie Baer; an updated reprint of *The Floodgates of Anarchy*; the autobiography and political writings of former Black Panther and class war prisoner Lorenzo Kom'boa Ervin, and much, much more. As well as working on the new AK Press Audio series, we are also working to set up a new pamphlet series, both to reprint long neglected classics and to present new material in a cheap, accessible format.

Friends of AK Press is a way in which you can directly help us try to realize many more such projects, much faster. Friends pay a minimum of $15/£10 per month into our AK Press account. All moneys received go directly into our publishing. In return, Friends receive (for the duration of their membership), automatically, as and when they appear, one copy free of every new AK Press title. Secondly, they are also entitled to 10 percent discount on everything featured in the current AK Distribution mail-order catalog (upwards of 3,000 titles), on any and every order. **Friends,** if they wish, can be acknowledged as a **Friend** in all new AK Press titles.

To find out more on how to contribute to Friends of AK Press, and for a Friends order form, please do write to:

AK Press
PO Box 40682
San Francisco, CA
94140-0682

AK Press
22 Lutton Place
Edinburgh, Scotland
EH8 9PE

SOCIAL ANARCHISM OR LIFESTYLE ANARCHISM: AN UNBRIDGEABLE CHASM by Murray Bookchin; ISBN 1 873176 83 X; 96pp two color cover, perfect bound 5-1/2 x 8-1/2; £5.95/£7.95.This book asks — and tries to answer — several basic questions that affect all Leftists today. Will anarchism remain a revolutionary social movement or become a chic boutique lifestyle subculture? Will its primary goals be the complete transformation of a hierarchical, class, and irrational society into a lib-

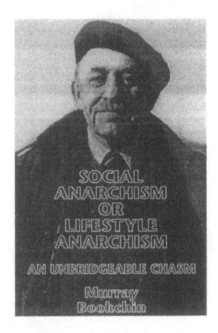

ertarian communist one? Or will it become an ideology focused on personnel well-being, spiritual redemption, and self-realization within the existing society?

In an era of privatism, kicks, introversion, and post-modernist nihilism, Murray Bookchin forcefully examines the growing nihilistic trends that threaten to undermine the revolutionary tradition of anarchism and co-opt its fragments into a harmless personalistic, yuppie ideology of social accommodation that presents no threat to the existing powers that be. This small book, tightly reasoned and documented, should be of interest to all radicals in the "postmodern age," socialists as well as anarchists, for whom the Left seems in hopeless disarray. Includes the essay The Left That Was.

ECOFASCISM: LESSONS FROM THE GERMAN EXPERIENCE by Janet Biehl and Peter Staudenmaier. ISBN 1 873176 73 2; 80pp, two color cover, perfect bound 5-1/2 x 8-1/2; £5.00/$7.00. Includes two essays, "Fascist Ideology: The Green Wing of the Nazi Party and its Historial Anatecedents" and "Ecology and the Modernization of Fascism in the German Ul-tra-Right," along with a new introduction. "Taken together, these essays ex-amine aspects of German fascism, past and present, in order to draw lessons from them for ecology movements both in Germany and elsewhere." [from the introduction] The reappearance of fascism in many countries of the Western world is one of the more disconcerting facts of the late twentieth century. Equally disconcerting is the attempt by fascist ideologists and political groups to use ecology in the service of social reaction. This effort is not without long historical roots in Germany, both in its nineteenth-century romanticism and in the Third Reich in the present century. In order to preserve the liberatory aspects of ecology, the authors, as social ecologists, explore the German experience of fascism and derive from it historical lessons about the political use of ecology — a problem that is of great relevance to ecology movements today.

Janet Biehl is the author of *Rethinking Ecofeminist Politics* (1991). As co-editor of the social ecology periodical *Green Perspectives,* she has translated a variety of essays concerning Green and anarchist politics as well as fascist movements in Germany today. Peter Staudenmaier is a left green activist who has been involved in anarchist and ecological politics in Germany and the United States for over a decade.

I Couldn't Paint Golden Angels: Sixty Years of Commonplace Life and Anarchist Agitation by Albert Meltzer. ISBN 1-873176 93 7; 400pp, two color cover, perfect bound 210mm x 245mm; £12.95/$19.95. Albert Meltzer (1920-whenever) has been involved actively in class struggles since the age of 15; exceptionally for his generation in having been a convinced Anarchist from the start, without

any family background in such activity. **I Couldn't Paint Golden Angels** is a lively, witty account of what he claims would have been the commonplace life of a worker but for the fact that he spent sixty years in anarchist activism. As a result it is a unique recounting of many struggles otherwise distorted or unrecorded, including the history of the contemporary development of anarchism in Britain and other countries where he was involved, notably Spain.

His story tells of many struggles, including for the first time, the Anglo-Spanish co-operation in the post-War anti-Franco resistance and provides interesting sidelights on, amongst others, the printers' and miners' strikes, fighting Blackshirts and the battle of Cable Street, the so-called Angry Brigade activities, the Anarchist Black Cross, the Cairo Mutiny and wartime German anti-Nazi resistance, the New Left of the 60s, the rise of squatting — and through individuals as varied as Kenyata, Emma Goldman, George Orwell, Guy Aldred and Frank Ridley — all of which have crowded out not only his story, but his life too.

"If I can't have a revolution, what is there to dance about?" — Albert Meltzer

Televisionaries: The Red Army Faction Story 1963-1993 by Tom Vague. ISBN 1 873176 47 3; 112pp, three-color laminated cover, perfect bound 5-1/2 x 8-1/2; $6.95/£4.50. An irreverent chronological history and analysis of the terrorist group that have shot and bombed their way through the last three decades of Western capitalism. From student radicalism to Stammheim to Euroterrorism,

this is the only book in print which charts the rise and rise of the armed guerrilla group that launched a thousand t-shirts.

A revised and expanded version of the near legendary Televisionaries issue of *Vague*, it romps through not only the RAF, but the June 2nd Movement, Red Brigades, Action Directe, the Revolutionary Cells and the CCC, bringing a barbed pop-culture view to the most explosive events of the last thirty years. Profusely illustrated throughout, with over thirty photographs and cool graphics with guns. Tom Vague is the editor of Vague, the **only** magazine ever worth reading.

> "Learning about wars, exploitations and oppressions in the same way as they learnt about fictional victims, they felt strongly not because they were a generation of visionaries, but because they were a generation of Televisionaries."
> — Jillian Beck *Hitler's Children*, 1977

> "*It was all very vague. We talked about Vietnam and then we moved onto other things. . . .*"
> — Hans-Joachim Klein

STEALWORKS: The Graphic Details of John Yates. Foreword by Jello Biafra. ISBN 1 873176 51 1; 8.5 x 11 inches; 136 pp; binding perfect bound, laminated cover; $11.95/£7.95. **STEALWORKS** is a loose collection of work created to date by self-described "visual media mechanic, image manipulator and graphic surgeon" John Yates. His work, a mixture of bold  visuals, minimalist to-the-point social commentary, and disturbing realism, involves the manipulation and reinterpretation of a culture-out-of-control's media imagery.

For the last five years he has acted as self-editor and publisher of the magazine *Punchline,* an ongoing series of sociopolitical graphic publications. The core of this book comprises the visual assaults he has created for *Punchline.* His work has appeared in several other self-produced printed projects, various small press publications, on t-shirts, and numerous record covers and other music related material. The collection is culled from all of his previously published work, as well as selective new and unpublished material. John Yates is a graphic artist and the visual mechanic for the independent record label *Alternative Tentacles Records.* He is currently working . . .

"John could make millions designing commercial magazine ads but instead aims his skills at unmasking and destroying those very mechanisms used to keep society obedient and asleep."
— **Jello Biafra,** from his introduction

END TIME: NOTES ON THE APOCALYPSE by G.A. Matiasz. 1-873176-96-1; 320pp, full color cover, perfect bound 5-1/2 x 8-1/2; $8.00/£5.95. **Straight from tomorrow's headlines!** Is it just sex, drugs and rock'n'roll in the year 2007? Hardly! *End Time* is the first novel by G.A. Matiasz. The United States is fighting a sophisticated, high tech counter-insurgency war in southern Mexico, against a popular revolution claiming the tradition of

Zapata. A military draft has been reinstated, and a strong anti-war movement flourishes in the American streets. The city of Oakland rises in anger, becoming the 21st Century's Paris Commune. In Alabaster, a small town north of San Francisco, the protagonist, Greg Kovinski, and a group of anti-war college students, gain possession of enough bomb grade riemanium to build a nuclear weapon several times more powerful than the one detonated over Nagasaki. Against the backdrop of civil unrest, Greg and his friends struggle to "do the right thing" with their deadly powers.

> "*A compulsively readable thriller combined with a very smart meditation on the near-future of anarchism,* End Time *proves once again that Sci-Fi is our only literature of ideas.*"
>
> — Hakim Bey

G.A. Matiasz writes a regular column of news analysis and political commentary for *Maximum Rock'n'Roll* under the name "Lefty" Hooligan.

A new CD recording from AK Press

NOAM CHOMSKY
THE CLINTON VISION

AK Audio, the newly formed audio imprint of AK Press, was created in order to bring the excitement and immediacy of the spoken word to people who care about politics. Reasonably priced, timely, and available on high-quality compact disc, **AK Audio** recordings deliver the best in political speech.

As an inaugural release, **AK Audio** makes Noam Chomsky, popular speaker, linguist, author, and political commentator, available to the home audience for the first time ever on compact disc. In 1992 Bill Clinton was elected President of the United States. After 12 years of a Republican White House, voters hungry for change believed Clinton when he promised a new vision, a new activism, and a new direction for the US. In **The Clinton Vision**, Noam Chomsky speaks about the US President's actions on NAFTA, health care, crime, labor relations, foreign policy, and the economy.

> *"Chomsky has been unrelenting in his attacks on the American hierarchy. . . . [He] is up there with Thoreau and Emerson in the literature of rebellion."*
> — *Rolling Stone*

> *"If the job of a rebel is to tear down the old and prepare for the new, then this is Noam Chomsky, a 'rebel without a pause,' the 'Elvis of academia. . . .' As rock 'n roll in the 90s continues to be gagged, it is ironic that a man of 65 years turns out to be the real rebel spirit."*
> — U2's Bono

> *"How adroitly [Chomsky] cuts through the crap and actually says something."* — *Village Voice*

ISBN 1-873176-92-9; $12.98/£10.99; CD; 56 minutes; two-color cover. **The Clinton Vision** CD is available direct from AK Press for $12.98/£10.99 ppd.